ALL GOD'S CHILDREN

D1421611

Books by Joni Eareckson Tada . . .

Joni
A Step Further
Choices . . . Changes

ALL GOD'S CHILDREN

Ministry to the Disabled

Gene Newman
Joni Eareckson Tada

Marshall Pickering

Pickering and Inglis
Marshall Pickering
3 Beggarwood Lane, Basingstoke, Hants RG23 7LP, UK

Copyright © 1981, 1987 by Joni and friends, Inc.

First published in U.S.A. by Zondervan Publishing House, 1987.
First published in the U.K. by Pickering and Inglis Ltd., 1987.
Part of the Marshall Pickering Holdings Group
A subsidiary of the Zondervan Corporation

All Scripture quotations, unless otherwise noted, are taken from the HOLY BIBLE: NEW INTERNATIONAL VERSION.

Marshall Pickering would like to thank the following for their aid in compiling the UK resource lists: A Cause for Concern, The Hard of Hearing Christian Fellowship, John Grooms Association for the Disabled, Torch Trust for the Blind.

ISBN: 0 7208 0720 4

Printed in Great Britain by Camelot Press Ltd., Shirley, Southampton

To Dr. Sam Britten,
with gratitude for his spiritual leadership
and his unending concern for the disabled community

Contents

Acknowledgments

In 1977, I left the safe and comfortable world of Public Education to work for a fledgling organization; ACAMPAR (Spanish verb meaning "to camp") was created to provide Christian Camping and Recreational programs for handicapped individuals. Through this ministry, the gospel was presented to hundreds of handicapped young persons and we sought increasingly to find a church home for these young christians where they could be ministered to.

This book was first developed as a seminar syllabus while I was employed by ACAMPAR Programs, Inc. Because of the increasing demand and need for a publication of this nature, the ACAMPAR Board of Trustees gave Joni and Friends, Inc. the publication rights for *All God's Children*. It was the prayer of the ACAMPAR Board of Trustees that *All God's Children* would be a practical tool for pastors and church workers interested in ministering to the handicapped community.

I want to express my gratitude to the ACAMPAR Board of Trustees for their encouragement to develop a resource guide of this nature. A special thank-you is also in order to Pat Hamman for his support, leadership, optimism, and commitment to excellence.

Many others have played a part in the development of *All God's Children*. Their faithful labors were indeed a manifestation of the dynamic and unified church of the Lord Jesus Christ. These individuals (too numerous to list here) will receive their just reward when they hear their Savior's words, "Well done, good and faithful servant."

Finally, I want to express my appreciation to Monique, my wife and co-laborer. Without her help, this project would never have come to fruition.

Gene Newman

Who Will Help?

Only weeks out of the hospital, I spent most of my time by the dining room window staring at the falling leaves, watching them swirl and sweep gracefully to the ground. I envied those leaves, for they could move. I couldn't.

Depressed and despondent, I knew in a vague, hazy kind of way that the Bible probably contained answers to my situation somewhere between its covers. But I was in desperate need of someone who could tell me what and where some of those answers were.

Shortly, God brought into my life a tall, lanky sixteen-year-old boy named Steve Estes. He had never so much as pushed a wheelchair, yet he was ready with a listening ear, a compassionate heart, and fresh insights from the Word of God. Even though Steve bumbled and stumbled his way around my disability, I was deeply impressed by his desire to help. And God used the long hours he and I shared over an open Bible to lift my spirits and turn my thinking around. I realized I no longer needed to make apologies for being paralyzed. God had reasons behind my affliction, and learning some of them made all the difference in the world.

In the time we spent together, not only did I gain a new awareness of God's sovereignty and grace, but Steve, as well, developed a new awareness of disabilities and the everyday handicaps that go along with them. As a friend, he learned how to hold a glass of soda to my mouth, push my wheelchair, or empty my leg bag. These simple tasks changed how he perceived the needs of the rest of the disabled community.

As I look back on my friendship with this young man, I am more convinced than ever of the desperate need of many who spend, as I did, aimless days wishing for a better life and hoping for a chance to shake the "handicaps" that encumber them in their disabilities. These people need comfort and hope from God's Word and his people. And the Bible makes it clear that we, the church, are the ones who can provide what is needed.

As you can see, I personally was helped by a teenager well equipped in only two ways—a working knowledge of God's Word and a caring, compassionate heart. But what about others? Who will touch the loneliness of the young woman with multiple sclerosis in a nursing home? Who will assist the boy with cerebral palsy unable to leave his house because there is no one to help? Who will hand-sign a welcome to the deaf man who enters a church? Who will stay with the mentally retarded child while her parents enjoy an evening out? Who will widen a doorway or install a ramp for the wheelchair-user new at church? Where are the "Steve Esteses" who will watch out for these people, pray with them, build them up in their faith?

Could that person be you? You may balk at the idea or shrug your shoulders, thinking someone else would be better for the job. Or you could, with the best of intentions, wish the responsibility on others, fearing that through your lack of expertise you may do more harm than good. Perhaps you are frightened, feeling unqualified and ill equipped. Insecurities creep in. "But I'm not sure I have the time," you think. "That sort of work is beneath me," you reason.

Take heart. Those are honest and natural responses. And these same responses could have been (and probably were, at some point) echoed by my friend, Steve. But God smiles on those people who will, by His grace, push past their inadequacies or fears and use what small gifts and abilities they have for the benefit of those in need. People—those who need help and those who do the helping—are changed. And God receives the glory.

All God's Children will help you and your church discover where you fit in an outreach to people with disabilities. And this handbook of resources and information will help people with disabilities fit securely into the life of your congregation.

Who will be the one who will make a difference? I pray . . . I believe . . . it will be you.

> *Yours in Christ's service,*
> *Joni Eareckson Tada*

Introduction

The World of Disabilities ... or Is It Handicaps?

WHICH WORDS DO WE USE?

And now to those words—the words that make you squirm and wince, groping for the right language to use when confronted by a person who, through illness or an accident of birth, is different from you. I make it a practice to look through brochures and literature from other organizations that serve the disabled community, and I am amazed at the variety of words that are used to describe a person's condition or disease. It confuses even me.

In an admirable effort to dispel the social stigma that surrounds words such as *crippled* or *invalid*, some groups have coined contemporary phrases to underscore the positive perspective. There are those who prefer to call us "handi-copeable" or "handicapable." We are the "physically challenged" or the "mentally challenged." To some, we are the "special people." To others, we are the "physically exceptional."

My friend, Gloria Maxin, who happens to be disabled (or "challenged," if you prefer), has written an exposé that pokes fun at the baggage of words our society has invented about our limitations:

I've had a hard time accepting these modern euphemisms for various handicaps, such as "hearing impaired," "language impaired," "vision impaired," "motion impaired," etc. Hmm, I wonder if the immoral will soon be called the "spiritually impaired." Oh, I hate such words because they sound squeamish. I hear in them a horror to say and see our simple reality. They're Mother Hubbard words clapped around our nakedness with missionary zeal to make us respectable—and to cover our shame. So I much prefer the tough Old Testament words like "deaf," "dumb," or "crippled" that tell the plain truth and set us free. Yet I'm a hypocrite of sorts. I'll refer to my plain fat with such euphemisms as "imposing" or "robust" or "substantial."

She has a point. In our great care to do away with prejudice in our semantics, perhaps we end up drawing more attention to the situation than we would have had we stuck with a good old honest word like *disabled* or *handicapped*.

Yet, are there valid differences and shades of meaning between even these two words? Dictionaries will tell us that "disability" is a word commonly used to describe a lack of physical or mental ability. "Handicaps," on the other hand, are any encumbrances that make success more difficult to attain.

Robert Lovering, a man disabled by polio, describes these differences in his book *Out of the Ordinary*.

I can conclude that I am always disabled, but I am not always handicapped. When I was a whole person and played basketball, being only six feet tall was a handicap, but I was not disabled. Working at my desk in my wheelchair I am not handicapped unless you ask me to reach a book on the third shelf over my desk. Therefore, in my condition, I am only handicapped when I try to accomplish something in which my disability makes success more difficult. Does the term really matter? I am what I am.[1]

And people are who they are—individuals who happen to have a disability. People are not to be labeled "retards" or "cripples" or "handicaps." They are people who happen to have a physical or mental impairment that may or may not handicap them as they go about their daily routines.

WHAT DOES IT MEAN TO BE DISABLED?

Somebody once said that although our bodies may disable us, it is often society which handicaps us. A disease or an impairment—light seizures, loss of vision, the loss of a hand or leg, a progressive condition such as arthritis or MS, mental retardation, or brain or spinal injury—can present problems. Yet many people control or at least manage their disabilities with either therapy, treatment, medication, or adaptive equipment.

However, these same people, with anything from annoying to chronic disabilities, may be severely handicapped if they lack an attendant or family member who can help with daily care routines. Handicaps occur when these same people are denied access due to steps or curbs, lack of elevators, ramps, Braille signs, or interpreters. One is handicapped by the attitudinal barriers of pity and fear. Even lack of transportation or employment, housing, or finances can present a handicap to the disabled person who desires to live independently. And, like members of the able-bodied community, disabled people are handicapped by sin.

You and your church can help persons with disabilities manage their way through a world of handicaps, freeing them to stretch beyond their limitations. People with impairments are whole people with desires and dreams, opinions and interests, vices and virtues. Life, full and rich with potential, is within the grasp of the disabled.

You can help the disabled population step beyond their handicaps.

Joni Eareckson Tada

Speed

Just as the dawn speeds through the night,
And dreams give way to morning light
(Which seemed so real before my sight)
So with the day I see and feel
Things which are true, joys that are real.
And when the shadows creep around,
These things won't flee, they will abound;
Because the truth of things is found.

Doris Dodge

Doris Dodge has cerebral palsy. Poem used by permission.

I
God Does Not Create Accidents

THE QUESTION OF "WHY?"

Ask anyone who has been awakened out of spiritual slumber with an ice-cold splash of suffering. "Why?" is often the question. "Why me, Lord?"

In reality, those few words are rarely spoken out of a heart that is honestly searching for answers. Initially, the question may be voiced in resentment, bewilderment, or frustration. A person recently afflicted with a crippling impairment or a progressive disease may clench his or her fist in anger against God.

There may come a time when these same people search through Scripture trying to discern the real purpose behind everything that has happened. Sometimes, though, they are unhappily forced to face a verse like Romans 11:33: "Oh, the depth of the riches of the wisdom and knowledge of God! How unsearchable his judgments and his paths beyond tracing out!"

OUR UNDERSTANDING IS FINITE

J. I. Packer, in his book *Knowing God*, tackles this problem of our inability to understand the purposes of God behind every event.

Now the mistake that is commonly made is to suppose that the gift of wisdom consists in an ability to see why God has done what He has done in a particular case, and what he is going to do next. . . . People feel that if they were really walking closer to God, so that He could impart wisdom to them freely, then they would discern the real purpose of everything that happened to them. . . . If they end up baffled, they put it down to their own lack of spirituality. Such people spend much time wondering why God should have allowed this or that to take place. . . . Christians may drive themselves almost crazy with this kind of futile inquiry.[1]

What makes us think that even if God explained his ways to us, we would be able to understand them? It would be like pouring million-gallon truths into our one-ounce brains. Even the great apostle Paul admitted that, though never in despair, he was often perplexed (2 Cor. 4:8). One Old Testament author has written, "As you do not know the path of the wind, or how the body is formed in a mother's womb, so you cannot understand the work of God, the Maker of all things" (Eccl. 11:5).

Yet, even though "there are secrets the Lord your God has not revealed to us" (Deut. 29:29, LIVING BIBLE), we are never lacking hope. There is an answer.

GOD IS SOVEREIGN

Let God's own words to Moses speak for themselves: "The LORD said to him, 'Who gave man his mouth? Who makes him deaf or dumb? Who gives him sight or makes him blind? Is it not I, the LORD?'" (Exod. 4:11). And hear the words of Jeremiah the prophet: "Is it not from the mouth of the Most High that both calamities and good things come?" (Lam. 3:38). The Psalmist says, "For you created my inmost being; you knit me together in my mother's womb. . . . My frame was not hidden from you when I was made in the secret place. When I was woven together in the depths of the earth, your eyes saw my unformed body. All the days ordained for me were written in your book before one of them came to be" (Ps. 139:13, 15–17).

Scripture indicates that not only is God sovereign to physical injuries or illness, but he is Lord over the changes and alterations that transpire within the womb.

Does this mean that God wants disease and injury? The key here is how we use the word *want*. God doesn't want disease to exist in the sense that he *enjoys* it. He hates it just as he hates all the other results of sin—death, guilt, sorrow, and catastrophes. But God must want disease to exist in the sense that he *wills* or *chooses* for it to exist. If he didn't, he would wipe it out immediately.

So God is neither frustrated nor hindered by Satan's schemes, but he permits suffering to serve his own ends and accomplish his own purposes.

THERE IS A PURPOSE

Although suffering is largely a mystery, it is not a mystery without direction. God has his reasons. Whether it is to mold Christian character, to stimulate empathy toward others who hurt, to refine one's faith, or to focus one's attention on eternal glories above, only time and wisdom will tell. The whole ordeal of our suffering is inspired by God's love. We are not the brunt of some cruel, divine joke. God has reasons, and learning some of them can make all the difference.

The following story vividly illustrates how God often uses the most unlikely candidates to accomplish his will. It is written by Gloria Hawley, who is the mother of two mentally retarded children.

"Psalm 127:3 speaks of children as a 'gift of the Lord' and 'a reward.' I didn't disagree with God, I simply refused the thought. Gradually, gently, God's light began to invade the particular dark chamber in my mind. Finally I realized that all biblical principles apply to all people. Each individual must respond, by an act of his will, and apply the principles to his situation. So I determined to administer large doses of God's Word to Laura and Craig.

"They seemed bored, so I began to sing Scripture to them. Craig became helpless with laughter, while Laura smiled politely and put fingers in her ears. It became apparent that the children needed the Scripture to be related to their own personal frames of reference.

"Laura and I began with the 23rd Psalm. 'Jesus is Laura's

strong Friend and Protector. He takes care of her in a very special way. Laura cannot see Him but He sees her. She is His darling little lamb.

"The paraphrase delighted and animated Laura. Her large, soft, brown eyes glowed and sparkled. Her smile was dazzling. Her attention span stretched as her understanding was kindled.

"A miracle occurred.

"Her teacher sent a note home: 'Laura is so animated; she is singing and telling the other youngsters, "I love you, kids! I love you!"'

"Her speech therapist called: 'What are you doing with Laura? She is responsive and bubbly!' My explanation was met with a cautious silence. Then—'If it works, do it. Send the Scripture along, and we'll work on it here too.'

"This shy, silent, fearful daughter of ours had begun her ministry—to teach me; to exhibit God's power; to bring God's Word into other lives.

"Laura particularly liked the end of the Psalm which, for her, stated: 'And some day Laura will go to live in Jesus' house and be with Him all the time! They will talk together, and she'll be able to tell Him how much she loves Him. No one will have to say it for her—she will be able to say it herself! Laura will live with her special Friend, Jesus, all the time. They will talk and sing and laugh together—with love. . . .' Psalm 23 is Laura's special Psalm.

"A few weeks passed and Christmas was near. Craig loved the story from Luke 2. Enthusiastic and responsive, he received the Baby Jesus with gusto. The miracle repeated itself.

"Craig's teacher called and, in tears, described how he had told his class about Jesus' birth—the star, God's love, angels and shepherds.

"Our little boy, his eyes shining with the light that split the heavens so long ago, spilled over with God's message of unchanging love—to a group of abnormal children no one had thought to tell before.

"Craig's ministry had begun.

"Craig and Laura remain handicapped. God has not chosen to 'heal' them. He is pleased to use them."[2]

Joni Eareckson Tada

Box 257

For all of us who are handicapped
I hope you will remember us.
Remember us talking outside and having fun.
Remember the man who can't see, laughing and joking.
Don't ignore us.

When we make friends we hold them in our minds
And remember the happiness we had.
Sometimes we make friends and for ten days,
  or nine weeks, or longer, we are close
But then it's funny how you forget us
While we remember you.

Sometimes the light goes out and you turn your back on us.
And I feel like a toy in a box.
Box 257, or 258.
You take out and play with me and talk to me
But there are no real feelings of love.
Nine weeks, and then "Goodbye, back in your box,
  I have new friends now for another nine weeks!"

What now for all of us?
Do you want us just to sleep and leave you alone
In our box on the top shelf?

John Hunt Kinnaird

John Hunt Kinnaird is a quadriplegic who suffered brain damage at birth. He lives in southern Chester County, Pennsylvania. Poem copyright © 1981 by John Hunt Kinnaird. Used by permission.

II
Tremendous Possibilities

A MATTER OF PERSPECTIVE

How should the church respond to disabled individuals? We could respond with despair, depression, and a sense of hopelessness . . . or we could view these individuals as the catalysts of great opportunity. The examples below demonstrate how one church seized the opportunity offered by disabled individuals and turned pity, fear, and avoidance into empathy, quest, and involvement.

THREE SUCCESS STORIES

What does a young man on a motorcycle, a woman talking on the phone, and a man moving chairs have in common? Plenty. All three of these people have been eternally changed as a result of their involvement in one church's Special Ministries Department. Meet my friends Rodney, Debbie, and John.

Rodney

Rodney is a young man with Down's syndrome, a condition characterized in part by mental retardation. He has been involved in a special Sunday school class for several years. One day after church I encountered Rodney, and we started to chat. Our conversation went something like this:

"Hi, Rodney. How are you doing?"

"Better than last week."

"What happened last week?"

"I came to church for the night service. After church, I got on my motorcycle, but it ran out of gas before I got out of the parking lot."

"What did you do then?"

"I walked the motorcycle down the street to the gas station, but it was closed. So I pushed the motorcycle all the way to another gas station that was far away. When I got there, it was closed too."

"Rodney, that was terrible! What in the world did you do?"

"Well, I got up on my motorcycle and started to pray. A few minutes later, a man in a car stopped and drove me to a gas station."

When Rodney told me this story, I was deeply touched. The living God was having an impact on his life. Instead of crying or panicking, he climbed on his motorcycle and simply trusted his Savior.

Debbie

Debbie has faithfully served in her church's Special Ministries Department for several years. In addition to being a highly organized, efficient, personable, and godly woman, Debbie is physically disabled. As a young girl she contracted polio and was left in a wheelchair, with only partial use of her arms.

Debbie's ministry represents an important principle that should undergird every Special Ministries program; that is, *our disabled friends should not only be ministered to, but also be permitted to minister their gift to the body of Christ.* Debbie's gift of administration and exhortation has had a dramatic impact on the congregation of her church. I hasten to add that, as a result of her ministry, Debbie has not only touched many lives, but also she has developed the self-esteem and dignity that comes through participation in the Lord's work. Additionally, by laboring alongside her able-bodied brothers and sisters, Debbie's physical differences have become less apparent, and her spiritual and nonphysical similarities have become increasingly visible.

John

John is a successful businessman who became involved in Special Ministries as part of a "package deal." His two teenaged boys wanted to work with the mentally handicapped, and Dad reluctantly tagged along.

John demonstrated his fear and ignorance one day when he stated, "I'll help arrange chairs and do some of the administrative work, but don't expect me to actually work with these people."

Over the next several months God did a wonderful work in John's heart. He began to see past his students' physical and intellectual imperfections, and he began to view them through God's eyes. John graduated from arranging chairs to teaching. He discovered that God gave him love, concern, and empathy for these special brothers and sisters.

A couple of years later, John rearranged his working schedule so he could have every Wednesday off. He started a Bible study at a nearby home for physically disabled young people and even developed a curriculum to teach them the fundamentals of Christianity.

John's story demonstrates how our Lord can take a self-centered and lukewarm Christian and mold him into a choice servant.

IN THE FISHBOWL

A ministry to the disabled community affords the church a wonderful opportunity to display God's magnificent, unconditional, and impartial love before the watching world. This truth is borne out by the experience of Grace Community Church of Sun Valley, California, which has developed a large Special Ministry Department.

This Special Ministry program was the subject of a radio interview with John MacArthur, the senior pastor of the church. The talk show host, who had attended Grace Church, was overwhelmed to find such a large number of disabled persons in the congregation. But he was even more impressed, he said, to discover how the disabled community are accepted by the leadership of the church. "Just the fact that they are there is one thing," he said. "But when the people in leadership embrace them, touch them, and talk to them . . . that's impressive, because you just don't see that." It goes without saying that if the leaders of the church show this kind of acceptance, it's easier for the other members to do so.

I find it fascinating to see how God can take a ministry to the "unlovelies" and turn it into such a visible, concrete, and powerful display of his love. The apostle Paul, in his letter to the church at Corinth, expressed it well when he wrote, "But God chose the foolish things of the world to shame the wise; God chose the weak things of the world to shame the strong" (1 Cor. 1:27).

In his book *Three Steps Forward, Two Steps Back*, Charles Swindoll eloquently supports this position.

> We're all faced with a series of great opportunities brilliantly disguised as impossible situations.[1]

Discerning the opportunities behind the disguise is the challenge facing those who desire to establish Special Ministry.

My mind has doors, and I was afraid to open them.
But when I did, I saw old friends.
Hurt, Love, Fear and Depression.
I said "Hello" to them and then
"Get off my back!"
But they didn't listen.

One of these friends comes when I am sleeping.
His name is Hurt.
Hurt says, "Think of girls."
And then he leaves my mind.

"Hello, Fear. What are you doing here?"
"I'm making you afraid to speak to girls."
"How do you do that?" I ask.
"When you look in their eyes you'll see pity
And hear it in their voices
And so you won't talk to them of love."

Now here comes Love to say "Hello."
"What do you do?" I ask.
"I give love to men and women, boys and girls
But they don't want to give it back to you."
And then Love says, "Okay. I'll give you friends
But they'll only tease you and walk out on you."

And so again I sleep, and with the morning
Come my friends to say hello once more.
"Friends, I'm fighting back. You can't control my thoughts.
I have strong medicine to help . . . Jesus."
He is listening, seeing, loving and helping me.
I speak to Him and He answers with what is best for me.

John Hunt Kinnaird

III

The Role
of the Pastor

A SHEPHERD'S TASK

The demands placed on most pastors are ever increasing. Consequently, when presented with the proposition of initiating a new program, a pastor's response will very likely be, "I think it is a worthwhile program, but I simply do not have the time."

Can this dilemma be resolved? Can a new ministry be initiated without adding one more burden to the already overworked pastor?

This problem is not new, of course; it has plagued the church since its inception. In Acts 6 it is recorded that the infant church was increasing in numbers so rapidly that the apostles could not continue to meet the needs of the congregation. Verse 2 tells us that the apostles summoned the congregation and said, "It would not be right for us to neglect the ministry of the word of God in order to wait on tables." Does that statement sound familiar? The apostles knew that their commission was to teach the Word of God; however, if they were to "wait on tables" (serve food to the widows), they would have to change their priorities.

The apostles resolved the matter by telling the church to appoint seven Spirit-filled men to be responsible for the distribution of food. This allowed the apostles to give themselves continually to prayer and to the ministry of the Word (Acts 6:4). John MacArthur, in his book *The Church: The Body of Christ*, has commented on this decision:

> The apostles were not being proud or lazy. They were not above visiting people. But they were establishing a priority for their own ministry. They saw that their distinct contribution to the Body was not menial activity, but praying and teaching the Word to equip the saints for the ministry.[1]

The pattern established in Acts 6:1–4 is monumental. God knew that a pastor could not possibly meet all the needs of his flock by himself; he needed help. The help comes from Spirit-filled saints.

The apostle Paul presents the same pattern in Ephesians 4:11–12: "It was he who gave some to be apostles, some to be prophets, some to be evangelists, and some to be pastors and teachers, to prepare God's people for works of service, so that the body of Christ may be built up." Paul is saying that a pastor can maximize his time by training Christians to carry out their own ministries.

John MacArthur has stated:

> Why do gifted men equip the saints? So that they might do the work of the ministry. The gifted men are to teach the Word to equip the saints to do the work. Teaching is the pastor's job.

> Too often, however, this biblical pattern is thwarted by church members who expect pastors to do everything. No wonder some pastors suffer so much physical and emotional fatigue. Some have been driven to breakdowns—they can't find the time to study the Word of God—because their church members expect them not only to equip the saints, but to do the work of the ministry also. That is not God's plan for the body.

> The local church essentially is a training place to equip Christians to carry out their ministries. Unfortunately, for many Christians the church is a place to go to watch professionals perform and to pay the professionals to carry out the church program.[2]

What can we conclude from this discussion of equipping? Several points can be delineated regarding the shepherd's task:

1. **Equip**	The busy pastor can maximize his time by teaching God's Word. This will equip the flock to do the work of the ministry.
2. **Inform**	If a pastor determines that there is a need for a ministry with disabled persons, he should inform the congregation.
3. **Pray**	The need must be committed to the Lord through prayer.
4. **Wait**	If it is God's will for a ministry with the disabled community to be undertaken, he will allow a leader to emerge from within the congregation. *It is important to wait for the right leadership.*

A SHEPHERD'S PERSPECTIVE

Because of its exceptional ministry to disabled persons, Grace Community Church serves as a model for other churches considering this kind of outreach. Pastor John MacArthur's response to commonly asked questions are most instructive:

Question: How did you view handicapped individuals prior to the development of your church's Special Ministries Department?

Answer: When I was in junior high school, I had a very close friend who was disabled. He was kind of spastic—I don't know the clinical term—but he always dragged one foot behind him and had to have special shoes. He was just mobile enough to want to participate in sports, but the other kids didn't want him on the team. The girls didn't know what to make of him, either; they just looked at him as kind of funny. But that boy and I were very, very close friends. He would stay at my house, and I'd stay at his.

That friendship did two things for me: first, it gave me a sensitivity to disabled people, and second, it removed the stigma of disability. Our relationship was also very significant in that I gained some valuable insights in helping him work through a lot of his anxieties.

This guy was my first contact with a disabled person, and after that, I never had any particular misgivings about disabled people.

Question: Did you have any fears or concerns about starting the Special Ministries program at your church?

Answer: No fears at all. I felt that this was a tremendous thing from the very start. After all, in his Word the Lord says, "When I have a banquet, these are the people I want to invite." It's his feast, his invitation. He doesn't leave anyone out, so why should we? You know, this kind of ministry takes you out of the cosmetic world where everything is perfect. These are real people with real needs just like everyone else.

Question: What are the benefits and liabilities of a Special Ministries program?

Answer: I have to be honest with you: I don't see any liabilities. Our disabled members give so much more than they receive from us. For example, when you see them sitting in wheelchairs and you know they've overcome all kinds of obstacles to get to church to worship God, you have to pray, "Thank you, Lord, for my health." They generate an appreciation for so many things the rest of us take for granted. And disabled people help us develop compassion—they make us want to make some active response to their need. They're the personification of "the little ones" our Lord spoke about in Matthew 18.

Question: Why should a church start a Special Ministries program?

Answer: First, disabled individuals are people made in the image of God. Forget the physical or mental disabilities. They are people made in the image of God—that's all. They are no less marred and no less capable of restoration than his other creations. Second, there is a biblical mandate that we not prefer one over the other. And third, the church is called to reach out to the poor, the needy, the destitute, and the hurting. If we believe the Bible, we have to carry out its dictates. But I don't see it as "grit your teeth and do what's right." I see it as a tremendous privilege. I think these people add a dimension of richness to the whole church family.

Question: How would you counsel the pastor who is considering starting a Special Ministries program?

Answer: In the first place, considering whether or not to start a Special Ministries program is a little like deciding whether or not a church ought to reach out to lost people. Deciding is really not the issue. As Christians, we have no choice. And if you try to second-guess whether you have the ability to handle it, you'll talk yourself out of it. God knows the needs of the church as well as your own strengths and weaknesses. You have to step out in faith, commit the ministry to the Lord, and believe it is right. If you do, God will supply the people and the resources and will send the Enabler alongside.

Question: With so many different kinds of disabilities and so many hurting people, where do you begin?

Answer: That question reminds me of a poster that we used to have in our church. It read: How Do You Feed a Hungry World? . . . One at a Time! Trying to figure out how your church could feed everyone in the world could cause mass panic! Just take one at a time. Start with your church families, including extended families, and you will likely find many disabled individuals among them. We've seen that happen over and over at Grace Community Church.

Question: What should the role of the pastor be in a Special Ministries program?

Answer: If the pastor is not completely committed, and if he isn't modeling his concern, it is going to be very difficult to get the people to minister to this population. I don't want to overstate my part, but when a visitor sits next to a guy who grunts and groans and maybe doesn't smell too good, he needs to see that the minister isn't uptight. Sometimes we have complaints about that kind of thing, and if a pastor isn't committed to obeying the Lord, then the pressure may become overwhelming. The pastor has to care about special populations because it is right to care. Then all of a sudden, you care because you care.

Make me a servant
humble and meek.
Lord, let me lift up
those who are weak.
And may the prayer
of my heart always be,
"Make me a servant,
Make me a servant,
Make me a servant today."

IV

The Role
of the Volunteer

When I was in the hospital, struggling to piece together the puzzle of my suffering, I desperately needed to know that the Bible was not avoiding the issue of my pain. Now, you'd think that God would have brought my way some smartly dressed, good-looking youth director to grab my attention and get me into God's Word. But no, as I shared earlier, the Lord had me spend time with another kid my age—a young boy with the spiritual gift of teaching.

Spiritual gifts are God's way of linking his body in love and action. In 1 Corinthians 12:5–7, we read, "There are different kinds of service, but the same Lord. There are different kinds of working, but the same God works all of them in all men. Now to each one the manifestation of the Spirit is given for the common good."

This boy, Steve Estes, used his gift to start me searching through Scripture and on to a life of meaning and hope. But other people used their gifts—unique energizings of the Holy Spirit—to inspire me further. The list of these gifts is found in Romans 12. But the list of people who can demonstrate the gifts is much longer.

The *gift of mercy* is one of those behind-the-scenes gifts, often administered away from the public eye. It's the lady armed not only with her Bible, but with a box of Kleenex, ready to console the lonely or comfort the hurting. It's that person who will touch or share a hug—someone who will sit and listen and pray.

During those lonely, fresh-out-of-the-hospital days of early adjustment, I remember one girlfriend who, during visits, would occasionally lie next to me in bed, hold my hand, and sing hymns to me. She didn't give me advice or a grocery list of Bible verses. My merciful friend simply used her spiritual gift.

Does somebody in your church have the *gift of service?* People who have the time, talents, and abilities can be the "hands and feet" of those who are disabled. One might drive a disabled neighbor to a medical appointment or on a shopping excursion. Perhaps the mother of a handicapped child needs a hand with all the extra household chores. A handyman with a heart to serve could construct a ramp or widen a doorway.

Let me give you an example. When I was first injured, neighbors would often call my mother and say, "Look, I'm on my way to the market. Have your list ready, and I'll be glad to pick up your items." These people didn't wait for my mother to call them. Instead, they pitched in and started using their spiritual gifts right away. Curiously, people like that didn't have an inkling as to how to push a wheelchair. They simply wanted to help.

People who have the *gift of administration* have the ability to envision success for those who are often too weak to envision it for themselves. They break down big goals into small tasks and, in the final analysis, enjoy seeing all the pieces come together.

For instance, I never dared to dream of going to college. Being newly disabled, there were just too many obstacles to overcome. Thankfully, another friend of mine used her managing skills to arrange for transportation to and from campus, volunteers to assist with note-taking, and students to escort me from one class to the next. I even needed someone to feed me at the school cafeteria. With the help of my friend and her special gift, I managed life on a college campus and, at the same time, dispelled many fears about venturing into public.

The disabled community can be benefited greatly just by people using their spiritual *gift of giving*. Adaptive equipment— new parts for wheelchairs, braces and crutches, seat cushions, arm splints, Braille typewriters, TTY telephones for the deaf, hearing aids, canes—is very expensive. Federal and state cut-backs in programs which assist the disabled population have brought these special needs to the attention of the private sector. By pooling free-will offerings, the church can demonstrate God's love in action by meeting special financial needs of certain disabled persons.

Pastors who have the *gift of prophecy* can rally the rest of the congregation to use their gifts in this unique avenue of service to the disabled population. Lay leadership is much needed, but motivation and inspiration must come from the pulpit.

First Corinthians 12:25 says, "There should be no division in the body, but . . . its parts should have equal concern for each other." And yes, disabled people have spiritual gifts too. Those who are blind, deaf, or mentally or physically disabled don't always have to be on the receiving end. We want to give to the church. I see my place in the body of Christ as one who exhorts and encourages others. Many people have used their gifts to help me; I, in turn, desire to reach out to them.

Even though I have the *gift of exhortation*, I don't consider myself a shining example. To exhort others does not mean you're some faultless, plaster-of-paris saint. A successful use of any spiritual gift presupposes the inability to be perfect. That way we may be sure that God's power will be perfected through our weakness.

You have a spiritual gift too. "Now you are the body of Christ, and each one of you is a part of it" (1 Cor. 12:27). Yet, with all these various spiritual gifts, there are some built-in difficulties. Different people will have different solutions to any number of problems. For example, somebody with the gift of mercy might want to sympathize with a disabled friend, while another with the gift of teaching might want to "sock it to him" with Scripture. One wants to console; another wants to convict.

How do people with various gifts function together in harmony? Paul explains in 1 Corinthians 12:31, "You should set your hearts on the best spiritual gifts, but I will show you a way which surpasses them all" (paraphrase). Then Paul begins his famous "Love Chapter," chapter 13, explaining how love will make it all work. "Patiently looking for a way of being constructive, not impressing or cherishing ideas of your own importance, using your gift with good manners, not pursuing a self advantage, not being touchy" (paraphrase). Truly, the Head of the church, Jesus Christ, is glorified when his body exercises its gifts in love.

A world of people need your assistance. And in a real way, you need that world of people. If we are to see the body of Christ at work in the world, all of us—able-bodied and disabled alike— must use our gifts. For our good and others'. For God's glory.

Joni Eareckson Tada

When they call me retarded,
That word's all they see.
Sometimes I think,
They don't even see me.

V
Mental Retardation

More Than a Name

Have you ever played the word association game? Sure you have. Someone says, "Black." You respond, "White." Let's play.

Word	Response
Tall	_____
Pretty	_____
Happy	_____
Mentally retarded	_____

What is your response to the term "mentally retarded"? If you were playing the game, the "right" answer is obviously "giftedness" or "genius." But life is not a game and, unfortunately, through the years I have heard and seen some distressing responses to that term. Some feel that mentally retarded people are mentally ill, deranged, lunatics, or sex maniacs. These misconceptions are the result of a general lack of understanding about mental retardation.

A more accurate response to the term "mentally retarded" would be "love." People with mental retardation are characterized by a tremendous capacity to love others. Their love is simple, and it is not contingent on reciprocation. It is the love of which Jesus spoke when he said, "Greater love has no one than this, that one lay down his life for his friends" (John 15:13). Certainly many of us can learn a great deal about love from our mentally retarded friends.

Did you pass the word association test? If not, you should spend a few minutes reading this section.

DESCRIPTION

Definition

The dictionary definition of mental retardation is "the lack of powers associated with normal intellectual development, resulting in an inability of the individual to function adequately in everyday life." In lay terms, mentally retarded individuals are "slow learners."

Causes

Mental retardation is caused by:

• Genetic defects
• Prenatal influences (disease, trauma, etc.)
• Perinatal influences (birth injuries, premature birth)
• Postnatal factors (disease, environmental deprivation, trauma, poisoning, etc.)

Classifications

The mentally retarded population is categorized under three major classifications:

- Educable
- Trainable
- Profound

Statistics

About 3 percent of the population of the United States is considered to be mentally retarded.

	Educable	Trainable	Profound
Abbreviation:	EMR	TMR	Profound
IQ Range:	55–79	35–55	Below 30
Percent of Retarded Population:	84%	13%	3%
Description:	able to learn, slow progress	able to learn self-help skills, socialization, and simple household chores	gross retardation, minimal capacity for learning
Academic achievement:	can learn to read, write, do math computations	can learn to recognize his/her own name, may be able to print name and address	may respond to minimum or limited training in self-help
Social achievement:	can learn to live independently in a community	can learn to behave properly, cannot live independently	limited social skills
Occupation potential:	can work in jobs requiring limited cognitive skills	sheltered workshop	requires complete care and supervision

Misconception

Mental retardation is not synonymous with mental illness and should not be confused with mental illness.

CHARACTERISTICS

Educational

A mentally retarded person generally has the following characteristics:

- Is easily distracted
- Reasons poorly
- Cannot grasp generalizations and abstractions
- Is confused by complexity
- Learns slowly

Physical

Mental retardation, characterized by limited cognitive ability, is often accompanied by physical problems as well.

- Poor motor coordination
- Heart disease
- Seizure disorders
- Visual impairments
- Hearing loss

The health histories of each mentally retarded participant must be reviewed, and appropriate attention given to those with physical problems.

Behavioral

The following behavioral characteristics are common among mentally retarded individuals:

- Short attention span
- Low frustration tolerance
- Lack of modesty
- Childlike mannerisms
- Normal sexual drives
- Normal emotional needs
- Interests that correspond to mental age, not necessarily chronological age

THE CHURCH

Why should the church minister to retarded persons?

1. **We are commanded to love.** "A new commandment I give you: Love one another. As I have loved you, so you must love one another" (John 13:34).

2. **We are commanded to teach.** "Therefore go and make disciples of all nations, baptizing them in the name of the Father and of the Son and of the Holy Spirit, and teaching them to obey everything I have commanded you" (Matt. 28:19–20).

3. **Salvation is possible for the retarded person.** Eighty-four percent of the retarded population is in the Educable category. Many of these EMRs have reached an age of accountability.

4. **Abundant life is promised the retarded person.** "I have come that they may have life, and have it to the full" (John 10:10).

5. **Parents of retarded persons need respite care.** Parents will need times when they are free from the burdens imposed by a disabled child.

6. **Social adjustment for the retarded person is commanded.** "Train a child in the way he should go, and when he is old he will not turn from it" (Prov. 22:6).

Many years ago a physician (under the influence of the Holy Spirit) wrote:

"When you give a luncheon or dinner, do not invite your friends, your brothers or relatives, or your rich neighbors; if you do, they may invite you back and so you will be repaid. But when you give a banquet, invite the poor, the crippled, the lame, the blind, and you will be blessed. Although they cannot repay you, you will be repaid at the resurrection of the righteous" (Luke 14:12–14).

God's Plan

God's plan for the mentally retarded is found in his Word. A careful study of the Bible will reveal answers to such questions as (1) Can they learn about God? (2) Are they held accountable? (3) Will God protect them? The following answers are not intended to be exhaustive; rather, they offer some preliminary insights.

1. Can retarded persons learn about God?

God can use the weak.

"But God chose the foolish things of the world to shame the wise; God chose the weak things of the world to shame the strong" (1 Cor. 1:27).

God does not show partiality.

"Then Peter began to speak: 'I now realize how true it is that God does not show favoritism but accepts men from every nation who fear him and do what is right'" (Acts 10:34).

"For God does not show favoritism" (Rom. 2:11).

The Holy Spirit discerns spiritual truths.

"God has revealed it to us by his Spirit. The Spirit searches all things, even the deep things of God. For who among men knows the thoughts of a man except the man's spirit within him? In the same way no one knows the thoughts of God except the Spirit of God" (1 Cor. 2:10–11).

God's Word will not return void.

"So is my word that goes out from my mouth: It will not return to me empty, but will accomplish what I desire and achieve the purpose for which I sent it" (Isa. 55:11).

2. Are retarded persons held accountable for their spiritual status?

Accountability is determined by an intellectual awareness sufficient to comprehend salvation.

"Let the little children come to me, and do not hinder them, for the kingdom of God belongs to such as these. I tell you the truth, anyone who will not receive the kingdom of God like a little child will never enter it" (Luke 18:16–17).

Those who remain like young children will not be held accountable.

Statistics show that 84 percent of retarded people fall into the Educable category. They will reach a peak mental age of nine to thirteen years of age; therefore, it is quite possible they will reach an age of spiritual accountability.

3. Will God protect those who are retarded?

God has promised to protect His "special children."

"Do not exploit the poor because they are poor and do not crush the needy in court, for the Lord will take up their case and will plunder those who plunder them" (Prov. 22:22–23).

HINTS

When working with mentally retarded persons, the following principles should be used:

1. **Success** Provide successful experiences. Those who experience success will be more willing to try new activities.

2. **Individualization** Gear activities, lessons, etc. to the level of the individual.

3. **Simplicity** Give simple and concise instructions. Complex commands will be confusing for the retarded person.

4. **Brevity** Plan activities for a shortened attention span. If proper activities and materials are utilized, a longer duration of attention will result.

5. **Examples** Use concrete examples. Abstract discussions should be avoided.

6. **Repetition** For maximum retention of a concept, use repetition. Repetition aids in impressing facts and ideas upon the brain.

7. **Reinforcement** Offer reinforcement immediately after a correct response is given. Verbal praise is generally the best reinforcement.

8. **Consistency**   When a proper behavior is exhibited, always praise the person. When an improper behavior is demonstrated, always correct the individual.

9. **Input**   Use a multisensory approach to teaching whenever possible, including the senses of hearing, vision, and touch.

10. **Firmness**   Be firm and loving. Retarded persons often need to be encouraged to participate in activities.

11. **Expectations**   Set the same standards of conduct as for nondisabled persons. *We do not help them by tolerating improper behavior.*

12. **Touch**   Communicate love and approval through hugs and pats. Most mentally impaired persons desire physical contact and will often respond to touch more readily than to words.

13. **Involvement**   Use higher functioning persons as helpers. They will feel challenged by the responsibility.

14. **Encouragement**   Allow retarded individuals to do things for themselves as much as possible.

15. **Prayer**   When praying with mentally retarded persons, use short, simple phrases. Ask them to repeat each phrase after you.

NEEDS

To minister effectively to the mentally retarded person, the following items must be considered:

1. SPECIAL CLASSES

The mentally retarded population has unique needs including the necessity for:

- Concrete lessons
- Continual reinforcement
- Repetition
- Consistency

- Individualization
- Instruction in following directions
- Instruction in socialization
- Instruction in self-help skills
- Multisensory teaching techniques

Recommendations:

EMR: The EMR individual should be mainstreamed into a normal classroom *if* he is capable of functioning in that environment. Note that assistants may be needed to ensure individualized instruction.

TMR: Special classes should be created for TMR individuals. However, it is important to mainstream TMRs into other church activities *as much as possible*.

2. TRAINED STAFF

In addition to providing a special class for the retarded, the teachers and assistants staffing the classes should be trained to develop the following competencies:

- An understanding of God's plan for those with mental disabilities
- A conceptual understanding of the physiological factors that influence learning
- An understanding of learning theory as it relates both to normal children and to the mentally retarded
- An awareness of existing curricula designed for the retarded
- An understanding of the biblical principles relating to the discipline of children
- An understanding of the biblical principles relating to leadership
- A knowledge of class management procedures

Many people feel that a person must possess "special" qualities in order to work with retarded persons. Any individual, however, who is allowing the Spirit of God to control his life already has these special qualities.

"The fruit of the Spirit is love, joy, peace, patience, kindness, goodness, faithfulness, gentleness and self-control" (Gal. 5:22–23).

3. CURRICULUM

The dilemma that presents itself to those working with mentally retarded persons of all ages is that most materials simple enough to be comprehended by them are designed for children. Try to imagine a hulking young man of twenty paging through a book illustrated with pictures of Dick and Jane! The image is incongruous.

It is important to provide curriculum materials that will not be demeaning to students. The resources listed at the end of this chapter include materials which have been developed specifically for the retarded.

4. THE CLASSROOM

The classroom should be:

- Located on the ground floor, since some of the class members will be physically disabled.
- Free from distractions (auditory, visual, etc.).
- Large enough to permit some physical activity.
- Well lighted and attractively decorated.
- Accessible to a drinking fountain and restrooms.
- Equipped with open shelves, cupboards, and bins for an assortment of toys, books, papers, crayons, and puzzles, as well as chalkboards, flannel boards, bulletin boards, and varying sizes of chairs and tables to accommodate the persons who will remain in the class from year to year.

5. MINISTRY

It is important to provide opportunities for the mentally retarded to become involved in Christian service. This will give them a sense of personal worth and recognition. In addition, they will be performing worthwhile tasks for their church, which might include:

- Folding Sunday bulletins
- Stuffing envelopes
- Setting up chairs
- Mowing lawns

In general, the mentally retarded excel at routine, repetitive tasks.

RESOURCES

General Insights

Senior, Robert. *Towards a Better Understanding.* Euromonitor Publications Limited, London, 1986.

The Human Horizons Series, Souvenir Press. Many titles on aspects of life, care and activity relating to mental handicap.

For In-Depth Study

Craft, Bicknell & Hollins, eds. *A Multi-Disciplinary Approach to Mental Handicap.* Bailliere Tindall, London, 1985.

Barton & Tomlinson, eds. *Special Education: Policy, Practices and Social Issues.* Harper & Row, London, 1981.

Mitler, Peter. *People Not Patients.* Methuen, 1979.

Clarke, A.M. & A.D.B. *Mental Deficiency: The Changing Outlook,* Methuen, 4th Edition, 1987.

From Christian Perspectives

Bayley, Michael. *The Local Church and Mentally Handicapped People.* Church Information Office, 1985.

Bowers, Faith, ed. *Mental Handicap and the Church.* Baptist Union, London, 1985.

Duncan, Leslie. *How Shall We Care? Helping Children With Severe Learning Difficulties,* Saint Andrew's Press, Edinburgh, 1980.

Lovell, Ann. *Simple Simon*, Lion Publishing, 1983.

Miles, Michael. *Christianity and the Mentally Handicapped*, Christian Brethren Research Fellowship, Occasional Paper No. 7, 1982.

Phelps, Caroline. *Elizabeth Joy*, Lion Publishing, 1983.

Wilson, Father David. *I am With You*. St Paul, 1975.

Wyatt, Grace & Langmead, Clive. *Charnwood*, Lion, 1987.

Young, F. *Face to Face*, Epworth, 1985.

Secular Resources

Association of Residential Communities for the Retarded (A.R.C.), P.O. Box 4, Lydney, Glos. GL15 6ST. Membership includes most major charities working in the field of residential care for children and adults with mental handicaps.

British Institute of Mental Handicap, Wolverhampton Road, Kidderminster, Worcs. DY10 3PP.
A professional organisation providing training for people working in mental handicap services; producing book-lists on specific aspects of mental handicap; supporting research into responses to mental handicap.

Campaign for People with Mental Handicap
16 Fitzroy Square,
London W1P 5HQ.

Downs Childrens' Association
12/13 Clapham Common Southside,
London SW4.

National Autistic Society
276 Willesden Lane,
London NW2 5RB.

Royal Society for Mentally Handicapped Children and Adults (MENCAP).
123 Golden Lane,
London, EC1Y 0RT.

Christian Resources

Providing Care.

Charnwood Centre. Charnwood is the name of a nursery centre which
gives handicapped and normal children the opportunity to play,
learn and grow together.
St Paul's Road,
Heaton Moor,
Stockport SK4 4RY.

Christian Concern for the Mentally Handicapped (also known as A
Cause for Concern)
118b Oxford Road,
Reading,
Berkshire. RG1 7NG.

The Shaftesbury Society
2a Amity Grove,
Raynes Park,
London SW20 0LJ.

Providing Information.

Baptist Union Working Group
Rev. B. George,
Baptist Church House,
4 Southampton Row,
London WC1 4AB.

Pastoral Office for Handicapped People
St Joseph's Centre,
The Burroughs,
London NW4 4TY.

United Reformed Church Ministry of Healing Committee
86 Tavistock Place,
London WC1H 9RT.

VI
Hearing Impairments

THE SILENT MINORITY

In September 1978 a thirty-three-year-old man, Joseph Heller, was found lying in the doorway of a partially vacant building. A passerby spotted his broken body and notified the police. Upon examination, the doctors discovered the man had suffered a multitude of injuries, including a severe neck injury, a fractured pelvis, several cracked ribs, and a broken leg.

The man had fallen five stories down an elevator shaft, pulled his bleeding body out of the pit at the bottom, dragged himself seventy-five feet through the dust and debris of the warehouse-type building, and had then waited for what seemed a millennium to be rescued—three days and three nights.[1]

What makes this story especially significant? Joseph Heller is deaf—a member of the Silent Minority which comprises approximately 0.5 percent of the population. His disability, accompanied by muteness, was the reason why he waited so long for discovery and rescue.

Just as Joseph Heller's silent call for help was not perceived during those eventful days in 1978, so also are the spiritual cries of the deaf unanswered.

Deafness is a subtle affliction. It does not attract much attention; but, like an insidious disease, the problems may not become apparent until there is a great deal of pain.

DESCRIPTION

Definition

The Conference of Executives of the American Schools for the Deaf has defined deaf people as "those who do not have sufficient residual hearing to enable them to understand speech successfully, even with a hearing aid."

Causes

Hearing impairments are caused from . . .
• Birth defects
• Disease
• Trauma (accidents)

Classifications

1. **Deafness:**   Total loss of the auditory sense

2. **Hard of hearing:**   Partial loss of the auditory sense

3. **Congenital deafness:**   Occurring at birth

4. **Adventitious deafness:** Occurring some time after birth

Statistics

A rough estimate places hearing loss among children at 5 percent of the total U.S. school population. However, only 10 to 20 percent of this group will require special education.

Misconceptions

There are many myths and misconceptions surrounding those with hearing impairments. It must be emphasized that deaf persons are *not* . . .

1. **Mentally retarded** — Hearing-impaired persons have normal intellectual capacities; *however,* they may lag behind hearing people in academic matters because of the language barrier.

2. **Physically disabled** — The hearing impaired do not always have physical disabilities; *however,* they may suffer from poor balance because of defects in the inner ear.

3. **Unfriendly** — Those with hearing impairments tend to congregate with others like themselves; therefore, they may appear unfriendly. *But if* we take the initiative in demonstrating a genuine interest in them, they will feel more inclined to associate with a larger group.

4. **Unlovable** — Hearing-impaired individuals are capable of expressing love; *however,* they are sometimes bitter or may lack self-esteem and, because of this, may appear to be aloof. *Therefore* it is important that we surround them with *agape*—God's kind of unconditional love.

DON'TS

When working with the hearing impaired, it is important that you consider the following suggestions:

DON'T . . .

. . . use the phrases "deaf mute," "deaf and dumb," or "deaffie." The correct terminology is "deaf," "hard of hearing," or "hearing impaired."
. . . yell or shout.
. . . cover your face with your hands or objects when conversing. Hearing-impaired persons often read lips or facial expressions as a clue to your conversation.
. . . use baby talk.

   ... allow others to interrupt you when conversing with a deaf person.

   ... pretend to understand when something is unclear.

   ... correct their English, unless help is requested.

   ... become impatient.

   ... ignore a deaf person if you are talking with a person with normal hearing.

   ... use "puns" or plays on words.

   ... talk too rapidly.

   ... hold hands while praying.

   ... tell jokes that exclude the hearing impaired. They may feel that the laughter is directed at them.

HINTS

The following hints will enable you to minister more effectively to the hearing impaired:

1. **Bring**   When you expect to be associating with hearing-impaired people, bring along a small notepad and pencil so that any questions or comments may be written.

2. **Relate**   Treat a deaf person as you would a person with normal hearing. Focus on common attitudes, desires, and interests. Emphasize the similarities between you, rather than the differences.

3. **Speak**   When conversing with a deaf person, address him or her directly. *Do not talk to the interpreter.*

4. **Ask**   If you do not understand what a deaf person is trying to communicate, ask that the statement be repeated or written down.

5. **Express**   Use appropriate facial expressions and hand gestures in order to facilitate communication with a deaf person.

6. **Look**   Maintain eye contact with the person with whom you are conversing.

7. **Wave or Tap**   Use a gentle tap on the shoulder or wave your hand to get a deaf person's attention.

8. **Approach**   Face the person and speak slowly, but not in an exaggerated manner.

9. **Sign**   Learn the art of signing. Many deaf persons rely on this method when communicating with others.

10. **Visualize**   Use visual means as much as possible when teaching the hearing impaired.

11. **Involve**   Use drama, puppetry, group discussion, and other techniques that encourage group participation.

FACTS

Some questions commonly raised in regard to the hearing impaired include the following:

1. Can deaf persons talk?

Most hearing-impaired persons have the ability to speak, but many prefer not to do so because of the poor quality of their speech.

2. Can all deaf persons read lips?

Lip reading is an art as well as a skill. Most deaf persons are not highly skilled in the art of reading lips, but rely on sign language in combination with lip movement.

3. Are hearing-impaired persons capable of advanced learning?

The average deaf adult has the equivalent of a fifth-grade education, but with the assistance of special education programs, many are capable of academic excellence.

4. Are hearing-impaired persons lonely?

According to Helen Keller, who was afflicted with both blindness and deafness shortly after birth, "Blindness separates an individual from things; deafness separates an individual from people."

5. Are hearing-impaired persons happy?

The average deaf person is lonely, frustrated, and unhappy, offering many opportunities for ministry. Those who come to know the Lord, however, can possess the fruit of his Spirit, which include love, joy, and peace.

NEEDS

Among hearing-impaired people there is a great diversity of hearing loss, communication skills, and learning potential. Therefore it is essential to deal with each hearing-impaired person according to individual needs. Those with sufficient residual hearing to function in a normal Sunday school class, worship service, or Bible study should be encouraged to do so. When a hearing-impaired person is unable to function within the mainstream of church life, however, special personnel and additional resources are needed.

1. INTERPRETERS

An interpreter trained in signing should be available for worship services. Be sure the interpreter is placed so that deaf members can see both the interpreter and the speaker. People serving in this capacity should have the following skills:

- A working knowledge of sign language
- Good understanding of the Bible
- The ability to translate on the level of the deaf in the community
- The ability to teach sign language classes

If a person with this competence cannot be found within the congregation, it may be necessary to train someone for this ministry.

2. SPECIAL CLASSES

A special class should be offered for deaf persons who cannot learn in an existing Sunday school class. This class will offer lessons adapted for the hearing impaired, with provision for dialogue and the varied levels of comprehension.

Consideration should be given to the following items when planning a class for hearing-impaired persons:

Size of class   A class can be formed with as few as three or four students.

Grouping	It may be difficult to group deaf persons of varying ages and needs. If problems arise, assistants may be required to ensure that each person receives individual instruction.
Teaching materials	Teaching materials should be highly visual and colorful. Pictures with captions are especially effective. (See resources at the end of this chapter for information related to Christian Education of the Deaf.)
Output	Lessons should be designed for immediate application by the students. Output can occur through role playing, response sheets, discussion, etc.

If there is only one hearing-impaired person, he or she could be included in a class of hearing students. Care should be given, however, to selecting the class in which the person will feel most comfortable. A special staff member responsible for assisting this student should be added to the teaching team.

3. TRAINED STAFF

Leaders should meet the following qualifications:

- Experience in working with the deaf
- Fluency in sign language
- An understanding of learning theory
- Spiritual maturity manifested by the fruit of the Spirit (Gal. 5:22–23)
- An understanding of biblical leadership principles
- A sensitivity to the needs of deaf persons
- A desire to minister to the deaf community
- An understanding of biblical principles relating to the use of discipline

4. BIBLE STUDIES

All believers need to be nurtured in the Word of God. Hearing-impaired persons may have learning problems. If this is the case, the church should consider beginning a Bible study designed to meet these special needs.

5. FELLOWSHIP

The church body needs to understand that hearing loss presents a communication problem which can lead to isolation and frustration. This problem can be overcome by encouraging members of the congregation to learn how to communicate with deaf persons. This can be accomplished in these ways:

- Writing on a notepad
- Using gestures
- Speaking slowly and enunciating clearly
- Learning sign language

Let us consider how we may spur one another on toward love and good deeds. Let us not give up meeting together, as some are in the habit of doing, but let us encourage one another—and all the more as you see the Day approaching (Heb. 10:24–25).

6. WORSHIP SERVICE

Some churches have started separate worship services for members of the deaf community. These segregated services have proven in many cases to be quite successful.

When separate services are held, it is important to provide opportunities for joint activities with other members of the church at large. The body of Christ was meant to function in unity. When the body is divided, it cannot function according to God's purpose.

The body is a unit, though it is made up of many parts; and though all its parts are many, they form one body. So it is with Christ (1 Cor. 12:12).

7. MINISTRY

All people, regardless of disabilities or hindrances, have been given spiritual gifts. Make sure that the hearing-impaired members of your church are given opportunities to use their gifts. If a Christian is not ministering by this means, he or she *will not* find total fulfillment in the Christian walk.

8. EQUIPMENT

As a deaf ministry begins to grow, the church should consider purchasing equipment to enable deaf members to communicate with the church. The Royal National Institute for the Deaf has all the details, but there are three options available at the moment (along with their variations):

Vistel. This is a telephone which enables deaf people to communicate with those who have the necessary equipment ie. a typewriter with screen. On average this equipment costs around £500. It is being superseded by other systems.

The Kuerty Phone, produced by British Telecom is the newest system devised. On average it will cost around £370 and will probably prove the most popular. It includes an ansaphone and can be attached to a BBC microcomputer.

The R.N.I.D. Telephone Exchange. This enables deaf people to communicate with a hearing person over the phone. All that is needed is a telephone, an ordinary TV set and a viewdata adaptor, approx. £190. (The R.N.I.D. offers a demonstration by appointment). A deaf person with speech difficulties can use his special equipment to type a message to the exchange, which will then contact the hearing person and speak to them normally over the phone.

For information about all these systems, contact The R.N.I.D., 105 Gower Street, London WC1E 6AH. (01 387 8033).

9. SIGN LANGUAGE CLASS

To encourage the church members to accept their hearing-impaired brothers and sisters, a sign language class taught by a trained interpreter should be offered.

RESOURCES

General Insights

Lysons, Kenneth, *Hearing impairment*. Woodhead-Faulkner, 1984.

I See What You Mean (Living with Deafness). BBC Publications, 1975.

Higgins, Paul. *Outsiders in a Hearing World*. Sage, 1980.

For In-Depth Study

Banford, J., and Saunders, E. *Hearing Impairment, Auditory Perception and Language Disability*. Edward Arnold, 1985.

From Christian Perspectives

Hassall, Philip. *I Cannot Hear you but I Can Hear God*. Hodder, 1986.

Secular Resources

Local authority social services departments and local voluntary organisations provide help for the deaf/hard of hearing:

Many social services departments have *social workers* with the deaf – details are available from your local Town Hall.

Many social services departments and/or adult education departments organise *sign language* and *lip-reading* classes.

National Organisations:

The Royal National Institute for the Deaf (R.N.I.D.)
105 Gower Street
London WC1 6AH   (01 387 8033)

The British Deaf Association (B.D.A.)
38 Victoria Place
Carlisle
Cumbria CA1 1HU   (0228 48844 Voice; 0228 28719 Vistel)

The National Deaf Children Society (N.D.C.S.)
45 Hereford Road
London W2 5AH   (01 229 9272)

The British Association of the Hard of Hearing (B.A.H.O.H.)
    7/11 Armstrong Road
    London W3 7JL   (01 743 110 Voice; 01 743 1492 Vistel)

Breakthrough Trust (Deaf/Hearing Integration)
    Charles Gillett Centre
    Selly Oak Colleges
    Birmingham B29 6LE   (021 472 6447 Voice; 01 471 1001 Vistel)

The R.N.I.D. publishes an Information Directory every year which gives a very comprehensive guide to where you can find help as needed, whether you have total or partial deafness.

Christian Resources

The following organisations aim to encourage deaf/hard of hearing people in their spiritual lives, as individuals, and in the setting of their local Church:

Deaf Christian Fellowship (D.C.F.)   Interdenominational.
    Paradise Street
    Rotherhithe
    London SE16 4QD   (01 697 0158 Voice; 01 851 6826 Vistel)

Hard of Hearing Christian Fellowship (H.H.C.F.)
    43 Stoneham Close   Interdenominational
    Tilehurst
    Reading
    Berkshire RG3 4HB   (0734 428988)

    The H.H.C.F. can provide information about installing a 'Loop' system to assist hard of hearing members of the congregation.

Church of England Council for the Deaf
    Church House
    Deans Yard
    Westminster
    London SW1P 3NZ   (01 222 9011 ext. 255)

Association for the Catholic Deaf of Great Britain and Ireland
    St Josephs Mission to the Deaf
    Henesey House
    104 Denmark Road
    Greenheys
    Manchester M15 6JS   (061 226 7139)

Blindness separates an individual from things; deafness separates an individual from people.

Helen Keller

VII
Physical Disabilities

To keep me from becoming conceited . . . there was given me a thorn in my flesh, a messenger of Satan, to torment me. Three times I pleaded with the Lord to take it away from me. But he said to me, "My grace is sufficient for you, for my power is made perfect in weakness" (2 Cor. 12:7–9).

Theologians disagree as to the exact nature of the "thorn" that the apostle Paul describes in his second letter to the Corinthians, though most assume that Paul was referring to a physical affliction of some kind.

Thorns come in different sizes and shapes. From the harmless prick of myopia (nearsightedness) to the devastating wound of total disability, every person who has ever lived has felt the sting of a thorn. Yet God's children have his promise of sufficient grace to conquer any trial they may face.

DESCRIPTION

Definition

Physical disability results from a neurological impairment (such as cerebral palsy or epilepsy), an orthopedic impairment (such as brittle bones or arthritis), or other health impairments (such as heart disease or asthma). The degree of involvement ranges from problems of minimal discomfort to severe, debilitating afflictions which interfere with a person's ability to function normally.

Causes

Physical handicaps result from:

- Birth defects
- Disease
- Accidents

Statistics

Approximately 3 percent of the population of the United States suffers some degree of physical disability.

Misconceptions

Not only do the physically disabled have to endure the pain and discomfort of their illness or ailment, but they must also deal with many popular misconceptions.

It is necessary to emphasize that the physically disabled *are not* . . .

1. **Mentally retarded** — Although some suffer the dual problems of physical disability and mental retardation, the majority have perfectly normal intelligence.

2. **Deaf** — Physically disabled people usually possess normal hearing. *Do not yell.*

3. **Emotionally unstable** — The physically disabled have the same emotional needs of those who do not suffer physical affliction.

4. **Uncomfortable when talking about their disabilities**

A disability need not be ignored or denied between friends; however, until you establish a friendship, show interest in him or her as a person apart from the disability.

5. **Unlovable**

Disabled people are just as capable of expressing love as the nondisabled; *however,* when a person is bitter, he or she may appear to be unlovable or incapable of loving. That person needs to be reminded that because of God's great love for us, there is not only provision for eternal life with him, but a unique plan for each individual in *this* life.

6. **Unfriendly**

A physical disability may result in poor self-esteem leading to withdrawal from friends and associates. That person needs to experience unconditional Christian love in order to learn that God's love is not contingent on outward appearances.

7. **Failures**

Physically disabled persons have been successful in many walks of life, including politics, business, and athletics.

DON'TS

When working with physically disabled persons, it is important that you consider the following suggestions:

DON'T . . .

. . . Pity them.

Uninformed people often pity those with disabilities. The disabled population needs love, understanding, friendship, and encouragement—not pity.

. . . Stare.

People who stare at a disabled person are forgetting that he or she has real feelings and needs. Instead, try a warm smile or initiate friendly conversation.

. . . Do everything for them.

Encourage a sense of self-sufficiency in disabled persons by letting them do as much as possible for themselves. Stand by to offer any assistance that is needed. Then depend on your disabled friends to let you know when it is appropriate for you to step in and lend a hand.

. . . Be impatient.

A person with certain physical disabilities may require more time in moving from place to place or in completing sentences. Allow the disabled person to set the pace.

. . . Ignore them.

Always acknowledge the presence of a disabled person. Attempt to include him or her in your conversation.

. . . Pretend to understand.

If you cannot understand what a person is trying to communicate, ask him to repeat, and listen carefully.

. . . Be afraid to talk.

Though communication with a disabled person is sometimes difficult, demonstrating the love of God through friendly concern will overcome all obstacles.

. . . Be afraid to touch.

The sense of touch—a pat on the back, a handshake, a warm hug—speaks volumes and assures the physically disabled that you do not consider them "untouchable."

. . . Be afraid to correct.

When working with young people, you can expect the same behavior from disabled persons as from any other group of the same age. Firm and loving discipline will let them know that you do not see their "differences."

. . . Talk baby talk.	The physically disabled possess normal intelligence and resent others talking down to them.
. . . Stereotype them.	Remember that people with physical disabilities are, first of all, people. Do not think of them as labels—cerebral palsy, polio, muscular dystrophy, etc.

ACCEPTANCE

In 1 Corinthians 12:7, the apostle Paul writes, "Now to each one the manifestation of the Spirit is given for the common good." Two important principles are stated in this passage:

1. Every believer has a spiritual gift.
2. Spiritual gifts are intended for building up the body of Christ.

From this passage we can conclude that disabled persons must be given an opportunity to use their spiritual gifts. If churches will encourage the disabled community to this end, two objectives will be achieved:

1. The disabled population will develop a sense of self-worth as they contribute to the life of the church.
2. The body of Christ will be built up.

Even the most severely disabled person can contribute by:

- Praying
- Caring
- Listening
- Being wise
- Being happy
- Maintaining a spirit of optimism and joy

As a leader you must help the physically disabled discover their gifts, encourage them to use these gifts, and then commend them when they have edified the congregation.

NEEDS

At first glance, people typically tend to focus on the most obvious differences between themselves and the physically disabled. Actually, when we come to know them better, it is soon evident that their needs are similar to our own. The physically disabled need love, fellowship, instruction in the Word, an opportunity to worship, and an opportunity to minister their spiritual gifts. They are more like us than unlike us! Therefore it is important to integrate these people into the mainstream of church life as much as possible.

> *There is neither Jew nor Greek, slave nor free, male nor female, for you are all one in Christ Jesus* (Gal. 3:28).

Listed below are some special needs of the physically disabled which should be accommodated, whenever possible, in a manner that will not tend to separate these brothers and sisters from other members of the body.

1. **Barrier-free access** — The physical church structure may be designed or adapted so that it is accessible to handicapped members. (See "Resources Related to Barrier-free Environment" at the end of this chapter.)

2. **Special ministry assistants** — Trained assistants should be available for such tasks as pushing wheelchairs, toileting, communicating, etc. (See ch. 10 for suggested skills needed by assistants.)

3. **Equipment** — A tape-lending library could be very useful for the physically disabled. Adjustable tables and ramps may also be needed to accommodate wheelchairs.

4. **Transportation** — Many physically disabled persons will need transportation to worship services, Bible study, and church activities. (See ch. 10.)

DISABILITIES

NAME	DESCRIPTION	CHARACTERISTICS
Amputation	Surgical: removal of diseased limb Congenital: limb missing from birth	Lack of function or mobility due to missing limb
Arthritis	Inflammation of joint	Limited movement at affected joint
Arthrogryposis	Persistent contracture of a muscle	Loss of mobility in affected joint
Cerebral palsy	Paralysis, weakness, or general incoordination due to brain damage	Increased muscle tone, uncontrolled movements, often accompanied by mental retardation
Cleft palate	Congenital fissure in roof of mouth, forming passageway between mouth and nasal cavities	Speech defect
Congenital anomalies	Term given to a divergency present at birth	Vary, depending on nature of anomaly
Cystic fibrosis	Respiratory and digestive system malfunction	Medication and inhalation therapy necessary to aid breathing and digestive processes
Diabetes mellitus	Inability to metabolize carbohydrates	Medication may be required. Often a diabetic needs to eat every two or three hours
Down's syndrome (Mongolism)	Genetic defect that causes mental retardation and various physical defects	Short stature, speech impairments, oriental-looking eyes
Encephalitis	Inflammation of the brain	Can cause brain damage

NAME	DESCRIPTION	CHARACTERISTICS
Epilepsy	Neurological disorder	Various forms of seizures that may cause unconscious and uncontrolled movements
Erythroblastosis (Rh disease)	Blood disease: destruction of red blood cells. A common cause of mental retardation	A transfusion at birth can remedy the defect. If not treated, brain damage can result.
Hemophilia	Blood disease: poor clotting ability	Minor scrape or bruise can result in severe hemorrhage.
Hydrocephalus	Increased accumulation of cerebrospinal fluid in ventricles of brain	Large head, usually accompanied by mental retardation
Legg-Perthes disease	Degeneration of hip joint	Special brace offers excellent chances for recovery.
Multiple sclerosis	Gradual degeneration of nerve pathways to muscles	Numbness, vertigo, gradual loss of muscle function
Muscular Dystrophy	Progressive degeneration of voluntary muscle functions	Frequent falling, waddling gait, difficulty climbing stairs, gradual loss of strength until walking becomes impossible
Osteogenesis imperfecta	Brittle bones	Minor fall can result in broken bones.
Poliomyelitis	Contagious disease caused by virus that attacks the gray matter of spinal cord	Possible paralysis
Rheumatic fever	Inflammation of heart, joints, brain, or all of these	Heart damage
Shunt	Anomalous passage or one artificially con-	

NAME	DESCRIPTION	CHARACTERISTICS
	structed to divert flow from one main route to another	
Spina bifida	Incompletely formed spinal cord	Paralysis, muscle weakness, and loss of sensation
Spinal cord injury	Trauma to spinal cord	Paralysis
Stoma	Artificially created opening between two passages or body cavities, or between a cavity or passage and the body's surface	Usually an external bag to collect body wastes

RESOURCES

General Insights

Peggy Jay Dip. COT SROT. *Coping with Disability.* Disabled Living Foundation   (£9.00)

Peggy Jay Dip. COT SROT. *Help Yourselves.* Disabled Living Foundation (£6.35)

> How, with family support, some independence can be recovered after suffering hemiplegis (Stroke)

Ann Darnbrough & Derek Kinrade. *Directory for Disabled People.* Woodhead Faulkner Ltd., Cambridge.   (£12.50)

> A wide ranging reference book of information and opportunites.

Disability Alliance. *Disability Rights Handbook.* 25 Denmark Street, London, WC2 8NJ   Tel: 01 240 0806   (£3.00, post free)

> Good clear information about benefits and allowances and how they can be obtained.

Christine Darby. *Keeping Fit while Caring.* Family Welfare Association, 501/505 Kingsland Road, London, E8 4AV   Tel: 01 254 6251   (£3.45 P'back inc. p & p)

> A fully illustrated step by step guide for carers.

Ann Shearer. *Living Independently*. Oxford University Press Bookshop, 116 High Street, Oxford, OX1 4BZ   Tel: 0865 242 913   (£5.00 P'back + £1.50 p & p)

The challenging stories of nine severely disabled people living in the community.

The Prince of Wales Advisory Group on Disability. *Living Options*. 8 Bedford Row, London, WC1 4BA   Tel: 01 430 0558   (50p)

Guidelines for those planning services for people with severe physicfll disabilities

Muscular Dystrophy Group. *Muscular Dystrophy Handbook*.   (£1.50)

A practical guide for those who suffer from Muscular Dystrophy and neuro-muscular disease.

A Burnfield. *Multiple Sclerosis – A personal exploration*. Souvenir Press, London   (£5.95)

A personal experience of living with Multiple Sclerosis.

Norman Croucher. *Outdoor Pursuits for Disabled People*. Woodhead Faulkner Ltd., Cambridge   (£8.95 + £1.50 p & p)

A book designed to introduce disabled people to a variety of outside pursuits.

Source Book towards Independent Living. (Care support ideas).   (£4.00)

One step On. (The experiences of 3 disabled people)   (£4.00)

Both available from Hampshire Centre for Independent Living, 31 Churchfield, Headley, Bordon, Hampshire. GU35 8TF

Bernadette Fallon. *So you're Paralysed*. Spinal Injuries Association, London.   (£4.50 inc. p & p)

Useful information on coping with spinal injury.

Collette Welch. *Spina Bifida & You*. ASBAH, 22 Upper Woburn Place, London, WC1H 0EP   Tel: 01 388 1382   (£3.50)

A lay guide for young people on Spina Bifida and Hydrocephalus.

Consumers Association. *What to do after an Accident*. P.O. Box 44, Hertford, SG14 1SH   (£5.95 inc p & p and bookshops)

A book about claiming compensation for injury and damage, and coping with the after-effects.

From Christian Perspectives

Eareckson, Joni. *Joni*. Marshall Pickering, 1976.

Eareckson, Joni and Estes, Steve. *A Step Further* Marshall Pickering, 1979.

Eareckson-Tada, Joni. *Choices...Changes*. Marshall Pickering, 1986.

Secular Resources

The Association of Carers, 21/23 New Road, Chatham, Kent. ME4 4QJ Tel: 0634 813981

Advice and support for carers.

Association of Crossroad Care Attendant Schemes, 94a Coton Road, Rugby, Warwickshire, CV21 4LN   Tel: 0788 73653

Works through local groups to provide relief and care in one's own home.

Association for Spina Bifida and Hydrocephalus, (ASBAH) 22 Upper Woburn Place, London, WC1H 0EP   Tel: 01 388 1382

Provides advisory and welfare services. Has local Associations and fieldworkers.

British Sports Association for the Disabled, Hayward House, Barward Crescent, Aylesbury, Bucks. HP21 9PP   Tel: 0296 27889

Co-ordinating body for sport and leisure for all disabled people. Information on all sports.

Centre on Environment for the Handicapped, (CEH) 35 Great Smith Street, London, SW1P 3BJ   Tel: 01 222 7980

Information service and publishers of architects designs. Library. Seminars. Register of architects.

Citizens Advice Bureaux. Please refer to your telephone directory for address of local office, or enquire at your library. In case of difficulty contact: National Association of Citizens Advice Bureaux, Middleton House, 115/123 Pentonville Road, London, N1 9LZ Tel: 01 833 2181

Advice on benefits, housing and legal matters.

Department of Health and Social Security (DHSS) Telephone Service: Freeline 0800 666 555 Out of office hours answering service.

Advice and information on Social Security related matters.

Disabled Drivers Association, Reg. Office: Ashwellthorpe Hall, Ashwellthorpe, Norwich, NR16 1EX   Tel: 050 841 449

> National organisation, provides advice on all aspects of mobility problems of disabled people. Has local groups.

Disabled Living Foundation, 380/384 Harrow Road, London, W9 2HU Tel: 01 289 6111

> A comprehensive information service. Working display of equipment and aids to support independent living. Information lists available, send s.a.e.

Greater London Association for Disabled People (GLAD) 336 Brixton Road, London, SW9 7AA   Tel: 01 274 0107

> Supports a network of Borough Disabled Associations. Provides an information service.

Leonard Cheshire Foundation, 26/29 Maunsel Street, London, SW1P 2QN   Tel: 01 828 1822

> Provides residential homes and family support services to enable disabled people to remain in the community.

Muscular Dystrophy Group, 35 Macaulay Road, London, SW4 0QP Tel: 01 720 8055

> A practical guide for those who suffer from muscular dystrophy and neuro-muscular disease.

Multiple Sclerosis Society, 25 Effie Road, London, SW6 1EE   Tel: 01 736 6267

> Information relating to multiple sclerosis. Local branches. Promotes research.

P.H.A.B. Physically Handicapped and Able-Bodied, Tavistock House North, Tavistock Square, London, WC1H 9HX   Tel: 01 388 1963

> National network of 450+ social clubs integrating physically handicapped and able bodied people of all ages into the community on equal terms.

Queen Elizabeth's Foundation for the Disabled, Leatherhead, Surrey, KT22 0BN   Tel: 037 284 2204

> Provides assessment, further education, vocational training, sheltered employment, and holidays with care.

Royal Association for Disability and Rehabilitation (RADAR) 25 Mortimer Street, London, W1 8AB   Tel: 01 637 5400

> Co-ordinating body for voluntary organisations serving disabled people. Information services.

Spinal Injuries Association, 76 St. James's Lane, London, N10 3DF   Tel: 01 444 2121

> Central reference centre of information and expertise for spinal cord injured people their family and friends.

The Spastics Society, 12 Part Crescent, London, W1N 4EQ   Tel: 01 636 5020

> Has extensive facilities for assessment, treatment, training and education. Runs residential homes.

Christian Resources

There are a number of christian organisations who can provide help but do not operate solely in the field of disability.

The following details are a selection.

It is suggested that local church groups or fellowships should be approached, most will be found to be very helpful.

London Diocesan Board for Social Responsibility, 30 Causton Street, London, SW1P 4AU   Tel: 01 820 0950

> Christian Social Work Service – will direct enquiries to local units.

Shaftesbury Society, 2a Amity Grove, Raynes Park, London, SW20 0LJ   Tel: 01 946 6635

> A christian voluntary organisation – has christian centres mainly in Greater London. Also housing, hostels and residential care.

John Grooms Association for the Disabled, 10 Gloucester Drive, London, N4 2LP   Tel: 01 802 7272

> A christian voluntary organisation providing residential care, housing, independence training, holidays and information service.

Church Action on Disability C.H.A.D. Rev. John Pierce, Charisma Cottage, Drewsteignton, Exeter, EX6 6QR   Tel: 0647 21259

> A new organisation supported by all the major religious groups, aiming to increase awareness in the churches of people with disabilities as full members of God's family.

Talent Night

Jesus gives all of us things we can do.
    Stand on your head
    Play a horn or piano
I know a man who can make up skits.
And also some girls who can sing.
    I love to see you do what you do.
    I do my thing too.

John Hunt Kinnaird

VIII
Visual Impairments

BURDEN OR BLESSING?

The campfire had nearly consumed its supply of fuel. Only the luminous embers could be seen in stark contrast to the black of the night. The silence was occasionally interrupted by testimonies of praise from the campers:

"I thank God for the mountains."
"I thank God for loving us."
"I thank God for the fun day."

Suddenly a small voice rang out. "I thank God that I am blind. I will never see the filth of the world. The first thing my virgin eyes will ever see is the shining face of Jesus."

Implicit in that potent testimony is the hope of everlasting life and an imperfect body made perfect for eternity.

Roger Dyer, executive director of the Christian Fellowship for the Blind, has stated:

> Blindness is what you make it—a burden or a blessing. It can be a lifetime spent in self-pity and an eternity of darkness as well, or it can be the challenge of a lifetime, to fulfill your greatest physical potential in spite of the odds; and it can be the beginning of the greatest spiritual adventure of your life—and it can last for eternity. Christ has made it possible.[1]

Blindness can indeed be a blessing; however, for that to occur, the loss of vision must be replaced by the "Light of the World," the Lord Jesus Christ.

DESCRIPTION

Definition

A person is said to be "legally blind" if his or her central visual acuity does not exceed 20/200 in the better eye with correcting lenses, or the visual field is less than an angle of twenty degrees.

In simpler terms, a person is considered legally blind if he or she can see no more at a distance of twenty feet than someone with normal vision can see at a distance of two hundred feet.

Causes

The eye is much like a camera. Light passes through the clear cornea, the aqueous humor (a watery liquid), the opening in the iris called the pupil, and finally through the lens and vitreous, which focuses the image on the retina. The retina transmits the image to the brain as a nerve impulse.

There are four major eye diseases. Each disease affects a different part of the organ.

DISEASE	PART OF EYE AFFECTED	DESCRIPTION
Glaucoma	Aqueous humor	Obstruction to the circulation of the aqueous humor
Cataract	Lens	Clouding of lens
Macular degeneration	Retina	Central visual acuity is affected.
Diabetes	Blood vessels of retina	Hemorrhaging inside eye

Classifications

Visual impairments are divided into two categories:

1. **No sight**	No optic impulses received by brain
2. **Partial sight**	Partial-sight symptoms include:
Blurry vision	Vision of 20/200 or worse
Spotty vision	Caused by scars on retina
Night blindness	A condition in which an individual cannot see well in a faint light or at night
Tunnel vision	Peripheral vision limited to 20 degrees or less

STATISTICS

It is estimated that there are are about 6.4 million persons in the United States with some kind of visual impairment; that is, persons who have trouble seeing even with corrective lenses. Of these, 1.7 million are severely impaired. This means that either they are legally blind or they function as if they were legally blind. Only about 400,000 of the severely visually impaired population have no usable vision at all. By age, the breakdown is as follows:

Under age 20	9.8%
Ages 20 to 39	13.5%
Ages 40 to 64	29.5%
Over 65	47.2%

It is noteworthy that approximately one-half of the legally blind persons in the United States are over 65 years of age. This is because the diseases which are the primary causes of blindness in this country are usually associated with aging.

DON'TS

When working with visually impaired individuals, consider these suggestions:

DON'T . . .

> . . . treat the blind person as if he or she were retarded. Most blind persons have normal intelligence and will comprehend what you are saying.
>
> . . . yell! The visually impaired have problems with sight, not hearing.
>
> . . . be overly helpful. The blind person is inconvenienced, not incapacitated. With minor adaptations, the blind can participate in most activities.
>
> . . . address a blind person through an intermediary. If you want to ask a question, ask the person directly.
>
> . . . make unusual revisions in conversation, such as substituting the word *heard* for the word *see*.
>
> . . . pet a guide dog without the owner's permission.

HINTS

The following hints will enable you to minister more effectively to those with visual impairments:

1. **Offer**   It is always appropriate to offer assistance. However, do not be surprised if a blind person prefers to try most things himself.

2. **Ask**   If you are eager to help a blind person but are not sure exactly what to do, don't hesitate to ask how you can be most helpful.

3. **Touch**   A gentle touch on the elbow is the best way to get a blind person's attention.

4. **Lead**   If a blind person gives you permission to walk with him, do not grab his arm—let him take yours. He may want to walk a half-step behind you. From the motion of your body, he or she will be able to tell when you come to curbs, steps, or turns.

5. **Announce**   When you enter a room or area where a blind person is present, make it a point to speak to him or her as soon as possible.

6. **Orientate**   When a blind person changes environments (during a walk, for example), be sure to inform him or her of obstacles, inclines, or slippery or uneven surfaces.

7. **Adapt**   The visually impaired person will be able to compensate for the loss of sight if activities, lessons, etc., are adapted.

8. **Teach**   When explaining a concept to a blind person, use concrete examples and incorporate or refer to as many of the other senses as possible.

9. **Stimulate**   Humor and voice inflection are important when speaking with a blind person. These techniques will help to set the mood and will compensate in some measure for the lack of visual stimuli.

NEEDS

People with visual impairment have unique needs. With a little imagination and minor adaptations, however, a visually impaired person can participate in most church activities.

The following items must be considered to accommodate the visually impaired:

1. PHYSICAL PLANT

The following modifications in construction will enable a church to meet the needs of their visually impaired members:

Handrails   Handrails are imperative with all stairs.

Guides   For carpeted areas, end the carpeting two steps short of the stairway to serve as a warning to blind persons that they are approaching stairs.

Lighting   Some visually impaired persons have limited sight. For these, proper lighting is essential. For example, there should be adequate light at book level in all pews.

Remember that glare causes eye fatigue much more quickly in poorly sighted persons. Therefore, areas surrounding the preacher or speaker should be illuminated with soft, glare-free light.

For more detailed information regarding physical facilities, see "Resources Related to Barrier-free Environment" at the end of this chapter.

2. CURRICULUM

Sunday school quarterlies, Christian books, and Bibles for the blind are available from various sources. (See "Christian Resources" and "Resources Related to Christian Education for the Visually Impaired" at the end of this chapter.) Consider these guidelines for using various types of materials:

Large print Approximately 90 percent of all visually impaired persons can read large print (18-point type is the accepted size for the legally blind). Various materials are available in large print. However, materials not available in large print can be developed by using 18-point type on nonglare paper.

Braille Approximately 40 percent of all visually impaired persons can read Braille. (See resource lists for Braille materials.)

Tapes Approximately 20 percent of the visually impaired can read neither large print nor Braille. Generally this group comprises persons who have lost their sight later in life or are otherwise physically disabled. Tape recordings are extremely helpful to these people. Such tapes can be made inexpensively, do not require special equipment, and can be developed in a relatively short period of time.

Other materials The use of concrete examples is vital to the learning process. People learn through experience; therefore, multisensory teaching techniques will promote optimal learning. In the absence of the visual sense, it is important that the blind person be encouraged to use all available sensory means to learning. Examples:

Finger paints
Modeling clay
Salt and flour
Papier-maché
Mosaics
Collages
Handling of animals
Drama
Puppetry

3. EQUIPMENT

The following equipment may prove helpful to visually impaired persons:

Typewriter — May be very helpful to a blind person in a Sunday school class, since typing as a substitute for handwriting is an important skill for communicating with others

Large-print hymnals — Especially helpful for partially sighted persons

Braille slate — A traditional device using paper and a punch stylus, useful for writing in Braille by either the teacher or the student

4. TRANSPORTATION

Transportation may be the greatest obstacle confronting the blind. If the church is truly interested in ministering to visually impaired persons, this issue must be resolved (see ch. 10).

Since the visually impaired will require some individualized instruction, consideration must be given to staffing classes with visually impaired members.

Assign a helper to assist the blind person in these ways:

• Taking notes
• Assisting with arts and crafts projects

- Recording reading assignments on tape
- Reading to the student
- Transcribing material into Braille or large print

5. MINISTRY

There are few ministries that are limited to sighted people. Therefore it is important to encourage a blind person to become actively involved in service at the church. Counseling, evangelism, teaching, and prayer are just a few of the kinds of ministries available to the visually impaired.

RESOURCES

General Insights

Minton, Graham H. *Blind Man's Buff.*   Both out-of-print;
Rose, June. *Changing Focus.*   available from libraries.

From Christian Perspectives

Scripture Union *Daily Bread* notes in *Braille* available from
    R.N.I.B.
    24 Great Portland Street
    London W1A 6AA

    also available on *cassette,* with Scripture reading from Torch Trust.
    Hallaton
    Market Harborough
    Leics. LE16 8UJ.

Bible Reading Fellowship daily notes in braille.
    St Michael's House
    2 Elizabeth Street
    London SW15 9RQ.

Information packs on Correspondence Courses – simple, general and Bible college to certificate standard. Torch Trust for the Blind.
    Hallaton
    Market Harborough
    Leics. LE16 8UJ.

Secular Resources

Royal National Institute for the Blind (R.N.I.B.)
  224 Great Portland Street
  London W1A 6AA.

  General resources including students library (Braille &
  Cassette), and rapid reading service.

  Moon Branch
  Holmesdale Road
  Reigate
  Surrey RH2 0BA.

National Library for the Blind
  Cromwell Road
  Bredbury
  Stockport
  Cheshire SK6 2SG

Talking Newspaper Association of the UK
  90 High Street
  Heathfield
  E. Sussex. TN21 8JD.

British Talking Book Service for the Blind
  Mount Pleasant
  Alperton
  Wembley
  Middx. HA0 1RR.

Scottish Braille Press
  Craigmillar Park
  Edinburgh
  Lothian. EH16 5NB.

National Deaf-Blind Helpers' League
  18 Rainbow Court
  Paston Ridings
  Peterborough
  Cambs. PE4 6UP.

British Wireless for the Blind Fund
  226 Great Portland Street
  London W1N 6AA.

Partially Sighted Society
  Queen's Road
  Doncaster DN1 2NX

For local amenities, contact local
Social Services (Blind Welfare) Office.

Christian Resources

Bible Society: some braille Scriptures.
  Stonehill Green,
  Westlea,
  Swindon,
  Wilts. SN5 7DG.

Braille Bible Fellowship: transcription of Fellowship notes to cassette &
  braille.
  4 Redcliffe Square
  London SW10 9JZ.

Guild of Methodist Braillists: transcribing theological books.
  19 Brookfield Lane
  Churchdown
  Gloucester. GL3 2PR.

Guild of Church Braillists: supplies Church literature in Braille.
  83 Buxton Crescent
  Sale
  Greater Manchester. M33 3LG.

Association of Blind Catholics: assisting blind Roman Catholics to take a
  fuller part in the life of the Church.
  58 Oakwood Road
  Horley
  Surrey. RH6 7BU.

St. Cecilia's Guild of Catholic Braillists: transcribes Catholic books into
  braille.
  21 Elvin Crescent
  Rottingdean
  E. Sussex. BN2 7FF.

St. John's Guild for the Blind: a Church of England Society to bring light
  and fellowship into the lives of the blind.
  44 Abingdon Road
  Luton
  Beds.

Scripture Gift Mission Inc: some large print and braille Christian literature.
  Radstock House
  3 Eccleston Street
  London SW1 9LZ.

Torch Trust for the Blind: Christian Fellowship and literature for visually handicapped people – in braille, Moon, Giant Print and on cassette.
Torch House
Hallaton
Market Harborough
Leics. EL16 8UJ.

Accept to Understand

We know and see each other with blinders on
Boys and girls, men and women
Orange hair, white skin, funny speech, hurt faces.
And we write each other off because "they" aren't like us.
"Oh yes, come in and have a chair
But don't think you are one of us.
We'll tease you, laugh at you and put a name on everyone."
"Eunice is afraid."
"Tim is mouthy."
"Laura is pretty."
"Jack is thoughtful."
But what if I have all four traits
Have equal parts of fear, mouthiness, good looks
    and intelligence
What will you name me then?
Who are you to decide what I am?
Just accept me what I am and take me into your
    understanding.
How can we learn each other without being friends?

John Hunt Kinnaird

Jesus loves me
This I know
For the Bidle
Tells me so

IX
Learning Disabilities

I CAN'T

Robert Carpenter tells about a boy named Billy in his book *Why Can't I Learn!*

> Two anxious parents leaned forward in their chairs one day in the principal's office of a suburban elementary school and listened hopefully as the school psychologist outlined a remedy for Billy, their third-grader. Halfway through, the principal interrupted.
>
> "I'm sorry," he said, "but we've tried that already, and it doesn't work in this case."
>
> Little Billy was not learning in spite of a good IQ, a good school, an involved teacher, a concerned principal and dedicated but frustrated parents. The dilemma was regrettably familiar: "We've done this before; it's not the answer."
>
> The principal suggested Billy's parents take him for a physical checkup, only to be told by the doctor their child was healthy and would probably "grow out of his problem."
>
> The parents next arranged for private tutoring. They obtained the counsel of several other child psychologists

recommended by the school who attempted to establish better understanding between child and parents. These sessions served to ease the tension that exists when children who have the ability to learn do not live up to parental expectations.

And yet, despite all these efforts, Billy's attitude improved only slightly, thus aiding the behavioral aspect of the problem, but his learning disability remained unchanged.

Family after family hears the verdict: "The problem is that we've done this before, but it's not the answer. Something is missing." The acknowledgment of an unresolved problem is at least a step toward solution.

The problem is not borne only by parents. Children who suffer learning disabilities inwardly yearn just as intensely and even more so for success. They are frequently misunderstood when they use unacceptable, and sometimes destructive, attention-getting devices. Such negative compensating adjustments are cries for help caused by frustrating problems of underachievement in education.[1]

This story is not at all uncommon. People like Billy are found in all strata of society—rich and poor, black and white, genius and retarded.

DESCRIPTION

Definition

A learning disability refers to a specific disorder in one or more of the processes of speech, language, perception, behavior, reading, spelling, writing, or arithmetic.

In other words, a child is classified as having a "learning disability" when (1) he has trouble learning, and (2) when his learning problem is not the result of a disability such as deafness, blindness, or mental retardation.

Learning disabilities include conditions which have been referred to as:

- Perceptual handicaps
- Brain injury
- Minimal brain dysfunction
- Dyslexia
- Developmental aphasia
- Central processing dysfunctions

Statistics

Learning disabilities which require special remedial procedures affect 6 to 7 percent of the school population.

CHARACTERISTICS

The term "learning disability" is a label which encompasses a multiplicity of learning problems. It is important to understand that learning disabilities will differ among individuals. In light of this fact, the following general characteristics are offered:

1. **Normal intelligence** — The individual with a learning disability will generally have normal intelligence.

2. **Diversity of abilities** — The child will have discrepancies in his own mental development, with areas of strength as well as areas of deficiency.

3. **Essential learning processes affected** — One or more of the essential learning processes—perception, integration, expression—are involved.

4. **Identification due to educational disabilities** — Identification is not usually based on overt physical or sensory characteristics, but rather on educational deficits; however, subtle sensory or neurological problems may exist.

NEEDS

There are varying degrees of severity in the area of learning disabilities; consequently, there will be a vast range of abilities and needs among these people. Communication skills, academic potential, and occupational potential will vary from child to child.

Since children with learning disabilities have a nearly normal intelligence quotient, their academic potential is generally good. The teacher working with them will need to adapt lessons so that each child can learn according to his or her particular learning pattern. The following needs are present in the learning disabled:

1. EVALUATION

The learning-disabled person must be evaluated to discover his or her optimal learning pattern. Testing will reveal the child's strengths and weaknesses in visual, auditory, and tactile modes of learning.

2. LEARNING STRATEGY

A learning strategy built on the information obtained through the evaluation should be developed for each child. (The information may be available through the child's parents or school.) The evaluation will reveal the "intact modalities" (most efficient sense avenues) and "deficit modalities" (less efficient sense avenues) of the child.

The principle presentation of information should be made through the intact modalities, with the deficit modalities used to complement them. For example, if a child has a strong visual modality but a weak auditory modality, the primary teaching technique should be the use of visual aids, with teaching tools involving sound used to complement the visual instruction.

3. SELF-ESTEEM

The child with a learning disability is very often aware of the fact that he or she is not able to meet the expectations of parents and teachers, resulting in low self-esteem. The following suggestions will aid in instilling confidence and a sense of self-worth in the child:

Praise	Take advantage of every opportunity to praise the child.
Teach	Tell the child that he was uniquely created by God and that God does not make mistakes. In addition, God loves him so much that he sent Jesus to die for him.
Provide	Develop lessons which will permit the child to be successful. Goals should be set in light of the child's abilities.
Watch	Be sensitive to the climate in the classroom. Do not allow other children to tease the learning-disabled child.

For more in-depth study on dealing with self-esteem in children, read *Hide or Seek* by James Dobson (Old Tappan, N.J.: Fleming H. Revell, rev. ed. 1983).

4. CLASSROOM

The classroom environment will influence the child with a learning disability. If the environment is overly stimulating, the child will be distracted. Strive to create a quiet haven with only a few well-chosen pictures, charts, and visual stimuli.

5. CURRICULUM

Most Sunday school curricula are geared toward the nondisabled, while Special Education materials are developed with public school subject matter in mind. It is possible, however, to adapt the applicable Special Education methodologies to the spiritual training of children.

6. INTEGRATION

Children with learning disabilities can be integrated into regular Sunday school classes with some planning and forethought. Train a special education assistant to assist the teacher in adapting lessons and individualizing instruction.

7. MINISTRY

It is important to involve learning-disabled persons in a ministry appropriate to their skills and gifts. Serving in some way will promote the development of a positive self-image.

RESOURCES
General Insights

MENCAP *Interlink.* Royal Society for Mentally Handicapped Children and Adults,
115 Golden Lane,
London, EC1 0TJ

A London Directory of Services for families and their young children with special needs. This directory has a good general information section with useful addresses.

J. Male and C. Thompson. *The Education Implications of Disability.*
RADAR,
25 Mortimer Street,
London, W1N 8AB

A Guide for teachers, has a summary of many specific disabling conditions with some suggestions in respect of the attaching educational implications. Also has a section on organisations who can supply further information.

Family Fund. *After 16 – What Next?* Joseph Rowntree Memorial Trust,
P.O. Box 50,
York. YO1 1UY

This booklet is intended to fill some gaps in information around the time of change from childhood to adult life.

Meeting Special Education Needs in Ordinary Schools, 1984 – A union guide by National Union of Teachers (N.U.T.)

C. Orton. *The Child with a medical problem in the ordinary school,* 1984 Home and School Council

Haskell, Barrell and Taylor. *The Education of Motor and Neuroligically handicapped children,* 1977. Halstead Press.

Edited by P.J. Cotton & A. Sutton. *Conductive Education.* Groom Helm.

For first hand advice contact the organisation which deals with the disabling condition of your child or interest.

Secular Resources

A.C.E. Centre (Aids to Communication in Education)
Ormerod School,
Waynflete Road,
Headington,
Oxford. OX3 8DD   Tel: 0865 63508

For information and advice about communication aids used in schools.

National Autistic Society,
276 Willesden Lane,
London, NW2 5RB   Tel: 01 451 3844

For information and advice.

Royal National Institute for the Blind,
224–228 Great Portland Street,
London, W1N 6AA   Tel: 01 388 1266

For information and advice.

Centre for Studies on Integration in Education,
The Spastics Society,
16 Fitzroy Square,
London, W1P 5HQ   Tel: 01 387 9571

Centre organised by the Spastics Society to promote good practice in integration of education.

National Deaf Childrens Society,
45 Hereford Road,
London, W2 5AH   Tel: 01 229 9272

For advice and information.

British Dyslexia Association,
Church Lane,
Peppard,
Oxfordshire, RG9 5JN   Tel: 04917 699

For advice and information.

Family Fund,
P.O. Box 50,
York. YO1 1UY   Tel: 0904 21115

Provides financial assistance to families caring for a severely handi-capped child.

Invalid Children's Aid Association,
126 Buckingham Palace Road,
London, SW1 9SB   Tel: 01 730 9891

Runs residential special schools for children with speech and language disorders and gives advice and information.

Royal Society for Mentally Handicapped Children and Adults,
123 Golden Lane,
London, EC1 0RT   Tel: 01 253 9433

For information and advice.

National Bureau for Handicapped Students,
336 Brixton Road,
London, SW6 7AA   Tel: 01 274 0565

Offers information and advice on further education.

National Bureau for Special Education.
1 Wood Street,
Stratford-upon-Avon,
Warwickshire. CV37 6JE   Tel: 0789 205332

Body of teachers involved in teaching children with special education needs.

Voluntary Council for Handicapped Children,
National Children's Bureau,
8 Wakley Street,
Islington,
London, EC1V 7QE   Tel: 01 278 9441

X
Getting Started

FIRST THINGS FIRST

Before launching a ministry with the disabled community, proper planning is essential. This planning must include defining goals, training teachers and workers, establishing adequate emergency procedures, and resolving logistical problems of all kinds.

In their book *Strategy for Living,* Ted W. Engstrom and Edward R. Dayton state:

> Planning helps us move toward goals, but planning helps in many other ways as well. Planning is a way of communicating our intentions to ourselves and to others. "Do two walk together unless they have agreed to do so?" (Amos 3:3). Unless you have decided where you are going, how can I decide to accompany you?[1]

Proverbs 16:9 describes the proper relationship between men's plans and God's sovereignty: "In his heart a man plans his course, but the LORD determines his steps."

This chapter is written to assist in the planning of a ministry with the disabled community from the perspective of Proverbs 16:9.

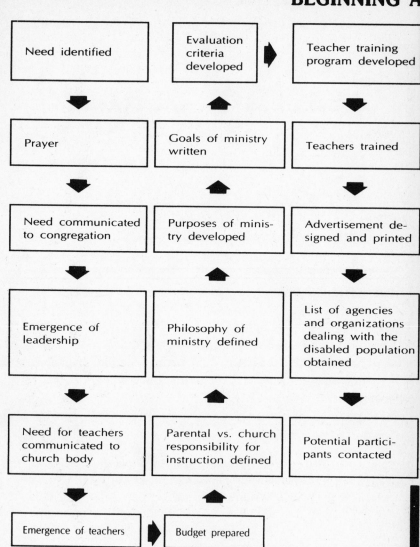

Need identified

→ Prayer

→ Need communicated to congregation

→ Emergence of leadership

→ Need for teachers communicated to church body

→ Emergence of teachers → Budget prepared

Evaluation criteria developed →

Goals of ministry written

Purposes of ministry developed

Philosophy of ministry defined

Parental vs. church responsibility for instruction defined

Teacher training program developed

→ Teachers trained

→ Advertisement designed and printed

→ List of agencies and organizations dealing with the disabled population obtained

→ Potential participants contacted

SPECIAL MINISTRY

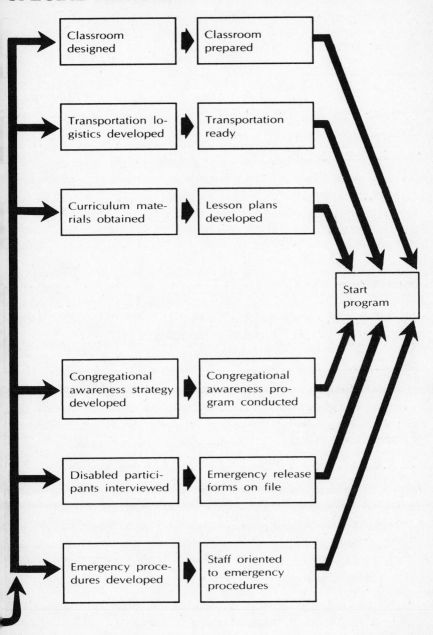

THREE PREREQUISITES

Once the need for a special ministry has been identified, several issues must then be addressed.

1. PRAYER

Any new ministry must begin with prayer. J. Oswald Sanders has said:

> Since leadership is the ability to move and influence people, the spiritual leader will be alert to discover the most effective way of doing this.
>
> To move men, the leader must be able to move God, for He has made it clear that He moves them through the prayers of the intercessor.[2]

2. COMMUNICATION

Inform the congregation that special ministry is needed, and ask for their prayers for the Lord's guidance.

3. LEADERSHIP

God will allow the proper leadership to emerge if the special ministry is in his will. If potentially qualified leaders do not come forward, then it may be concluded that . . .

- It is not the Lord's time for such a ministry.
or
- It is not the place for the ministry.

If, after prayer and elapsed time, the need is still perceived, prayer should continue.

If a ministry is initiated with the wrong leadership, problems may arise, including:

- Failure of the disabled participants to see God manifested in the lives of their teachers
- Loss of time, resources, and opportunity to minister to some of God's most precious ones

PHILOSOPHY OF MINISTRY TO DISABLED CHILDREN

1. PARENTS VERSUS THE CHURCH

In order to develop a proper philosophy for special ministries to children, the biblical standard for instruction must first be examined.

God's Word teaches that children are to be reared in the discipline and instruction of the Lord. The Old Testament instructs parents (Gen. 18:19; Deut. 4:9; 6:6–7; Ps. 78:5) and the Jewish people in general (Deut. 31:11–13) to teach their children God's laws. The New Testament reaffirms the Old Testament concept that parents are to train their children (Eph. 6:4).

If the Old Testament teaches that child rearing is the dual obligation of parents and society (the Jewish nation), then who should bear the primary responsibility? Howard Hendricks has stated:

> The average church has a child one percent of his time; the home has him 83 percent of the time and the school the remainder. We are too often trying to do in our churches on a one-percent basis what we cannot accomplish. We are neglecting this choice 83 percent period when children are exposed to parents on a very dynamic interpersonal level. The home marks the child for life.

Hendricks further states:

> Columbia University spent a quarter of a million dollars in research, only to corroborate the truth of Scripture. Conclusion: there is no second force in the life of a child compared with the impact of his home.[3]

Since the family unit is ordained by God, we can make the following assumptions:

- The primary responsibility for rearing children should rest with the parents.
- The church should reinforce the teaching of the parents.
- The Sunday school will assume greater responsibility for "raising up" children from non-Christian homes; however, in such circumstances the priority for the church should be the salvation of the parents.

For further insights into the roles of the parents and the church, read "Project–Proverbs 22:6," a booklet available from Grace Community Church, 13248 Roscoe Boulevard, Sun Valley, CA 91352.

2. SPECIAL MINISTRIES PHILOSOPHY

Scripture defines the goal of Christian education as a "trained-up" child. The child must reach a state of maturity in which he or she is self-disciplined, acting on the foundation of God's Word (2 Tim. 3:16–17). Ephesians 4:14 says:

> Then we will no longer be infants, tossed back and forth by the waves, and blown here and there by every wind of teaching and by the cunning and craftiness of men in their deceitful scheming.

This goal should be the same for any body of believers; however, well-meaning people often lose sight of that goal when working with the disabled community. Spiritual growth should be the thrust of *any* Christian education program. *Disabled people simply require an adaptation of teaching methods in their quest for spiritual maturity.*

WORKERS

A special ministries program cannot be successful without the proper personnel. Note the following considerations regarding recruitment and training of staff:

1. RECRUITMENT

Announcements about the special program and staffing needs could be made by means of bulletin boards, flyers, and church newsletters. To generate maximum interest among members of the congregation, recruitment efforts might coincide with a special ministries presentation.

2. QUALIFICATIONS

John 16:13 teaches that one purpose of the indwelling Holy Spirit is to reveal truth to Christians. The implication is obvious: to teach in a Christian environment, a person must surrender the control of his life to the Holy Spirit. With this fact in mind, consider the following qualifications for teachers of the disabled community:

- The teacher must have a personal relationship with the Lord Jesus Christ (1 Tim. 4:1; 6:3–4; 2 Tim. 2:2).
- The teacher must manifest a high level of maturity and understanding (Eph. 4:11–17; 1 Tim. 3:6).
- The teacher's life must give evidence of control by the Holy Spirit (1 Cor. 3:1–3; Eph. 5:18; Gal. 5:22–23; 2 Peter 1:5–8).
- The teacher's ministry must manifest the necessary combination of gifts to handle the assigned task (Rom. 13:3–8; 1 Cor. 3:5–9; 12:1–31; 1 Peter 4:10).
- The teacher must prove faithful (2 Tim. 2:2).

3. COMMITMENT

It takes time to become acquainted with the special needs of disabled students. Each is an individual; consequently, he or she will have unique physical, social, spiritual, emotional, and learning characteristics. To provide continuity for the students, teachers should be willing to commit themselves to a minimum tenure of one year.

4. TRAINING

A training program should be developed to equip the workers with the following skills:

- An understanding of affliction as it relates to God's will
- A philosophy for dealing with exceptional persons within the church
- An understanding of the unique needs of the specific population with which the worker will be dealing
- Knowledge of physiological factors which influence learning

- An understanding of learning theory
- Skill in preparing lessons which will promote optimal learning
- An awareness of existing curricula for special populations
- An understanding of biblical principles regarding the use of discipline
- Knowledge of biblical leadership principles
- An understanding of class management procedures

Special ministry assistants may be required to help with disabled students who are placed in regular classes. These assistants should have as many of the skills listed above as are necessary to assist those with whom they will be working.

5. ADULT/STUDENT RATIO

The number of teachers required to work with disabled persons will vary according to the situation. The following ratios are offered as guidelines:

Disability	Acceptable ratio	Ideal ratio
Mentally retarded	3:1	1:1
Physically disabled	2:1	1:1
Deaf	4:1	2:1
Blind	1:1	1:1

ADVERTISING

1. **Congregation**	Announce to the congregation that the church is starting a ministry to the disabled community. Members can inform friends, relatives, and acquaintances about the program.
2. **Residential facilities**	Distribute announcements at residential facilities serving disabled persons.

3. **Schools**	Distribute announcements at schools. Local PTA or other parent groups may be willing to publicize the program in their newsletter.
4. **Government agencies**	Many state and local government agencies serving the disabled population would be willing to publicize the program.
5. **Private agencies**	Many private agencies exist to serve the disabled. Contact them for ideas for advertising.
6. **Newspapers**	Prepare news releases and "community calendar" information for local newspapers.
7. **TV**	Television stations must donate a portion of airtime to public service announcements. Don't overlook this opportunity.
8. **Word of mouth**	If disabled people find their spiritual needs satisfied through your special ministries program, they will tell their friends.

TRANSPORTATION

Transportation is an important factor when planning a special ministry. Consider the following strategies:

1. INDIVIDUAL MINISTRY

Individual members of the church may offer to use their own vehicles to transport disabled individuals to the church for services and activities. The obvious advantages of this strategy are twofold:

- More people will become involved in the program and will become aware of the special needs and rewards of this kind of ministry.
- Since personal vehicles would be used, no capital outlay of church funds is required.

The disadvantage becomes apparent in the case of a physically disabled person whose cumbersome wheelchair might not fit into a standard passenger car. In this case, a large vehicle such as a van would be needed. With careful planning, however, this strategy can be effective, especially if a church member volunteered to serve as transportation coordinator.

2. BUS MINISTRY

Many churches have found that their outreach ministry has been enhanced by the purchase of a church bus or van. In addition to the expenditure of capital funds, this approach requires a trained and properly licensed driver.

The advantages in a bus ministry lie in the ease with which wheelchairs and other special apparatuses may be handled.

The disadvantages must be carefully weighed:

- Maintenance costs on the bus may be prohibitive.
- Persons who are picked up at the beginning of the route must ride for long periods of time.
- The exceptional mode of transportation may foster feelings of separation from the rest of the congregation.

GETTING ACQUAINTED

It is important to become acquainted with each new student. An interview with the disabled person and, if possible, a parent or close relative, should occur before enrollment in a special ministries program. The interview should deal with these subjects:

1. **Cautions**

The physical conditions listed below require careful monitoring and special instructions on how to react in an emergency. It is important to understand the limitations imposed on a person with any of these disabilities.

- Allergies
- Epilepsy
- Heart disease
- Diabetes

- Brittle bones
- Hemophilia

2. **Medication**   Medication should be given as prescribed. It is helpful to keep a chart of the medications and dosages required of people in the program, as well as proper written authorization from the person's doctor allowing staff members to administer medication.

3. **Appliances**   Many physically disabled persons must use orthopedic appliances such as wheelchairs, braces, or catheters. It is important to understand the proper use of these appliances.

4. **Unusual problems**   You must be aware of any unusual conditions that may require special attention.

Information about these items should be listed on an Emergency Medical Release Card so that the teacher will have access to pertinent medical information.

INTERVIEW FORM

Name: _____ **Age** _____

Interviewer's name: _____

Name of parent/guardian: _____

Physical disability: _____

Seizures?   ☐ Yes   ☐ No

How often? _____ Type: _____

Helpful hints: _____

	Yes	No			Yes	No
Allergies	☐	☐	Lung condition:		☐	☐
Heart condition	☐	☐	Special diet		☐	☐

Please note necessary details pertaining to the above:

_____

_____

_____

Precautions: _____

_____

_____

Medication information: _____

_____

_____

Medication schedule: _____

_____

Special appliances:

☐ Wheelchair   ☐ Crutches   ☐ Hearing aid
☐ Walker   ☐ Braces   ☐ Talking board
☐ Canes   ☐ Eyeglasses ☐ Other _____

Special care of appliances: _____

_____

_____

Behavior information: _____

_____

_____

_____

Assistance: Does participant need assistance with:

	Yes	No	Comments
Feeding	☐	☐	_____
Dressing	☐	☐	_____
Undressing	☐	☐	_____
Toileting	☐	☐	_____
Braces	☐	☐	_____

Additional information:

	Yes	No
Does the person fatigue easily?	☐	☐
Does the person chill easily?	☐	☐

Additional comments: _____

_____

_____

Signatures:

_____   _____   _____

Date   Parent/guardian   Interviewer

EMERGENCY PLAN

Because of the high incidence of medical problems associated with handicapping conditions, it is wise to adopt a plan of action for emergencies which may arise while disabled persons are on the church premises. Post the plan in strategic locations throughout the building, listing procedures to be followed in the event of a medical emergency. Communicate this plan to all people who will spend a significant amount of time at the church (staff members, volunteers, etc.).

When developing the plan, consider the following:

1. **First aid**

   A working knowledge of first aid is essential for leaders in "high risk" areas of the church such as athletics and special ministries.

2. **Emergency medical release statement**

   Keep on file a statement from the parents that gives permission for medical personnel to administer emergency treatment to minors.

3. **Emergency treatment information**

   Create a file of hospitals with emergency treatment rooms, doctors and local paramedics, with addresses and telephone numbers, including information about the disabled person's personal physician.

Here is a suggested emergency medical release statement:

SPECIAL MINISTRIES, _____ CHURCH
Emergency Medical Release Form

Name _____ Birthdate _____
       Last   First   Middle

Home address _____ City _____ Zip ____

Father _____ Home phone _____
    Home address _____
    Business address _____
    Phone _____ Work days _____ Hours _____

Mother _____ Home phone _____
    Home address _____
    Business address _____
    Phone _____ Work days _____ Hours _____

In emergency, if parents cannot be reached, notify:
    Name _____ Relationship ____
    Phone _____ Address _____

Disability _____ Seizures _____
    Heart condition _____ Lung condition _____ Allergies _____
    Stoma _____ Catheter _____ Shunt _____ Medication? _____
    Wheelchair _____ Crutches/cane _____ Braces _____ Other _____

Comments _____
_____

Medical Release

We, the undersigned, parents or legal guardians of _____ a minor, and said minor (if 18 years of age or older), do hereby authorize any adult person in whose care the said minor has been entrusted by _____ Church to consent to any x-ray examination, anesthetic, medical or surgical diagnosis or treatment, and hospital care to be rendered to said minor under the general or special supervision and upon the advice of a physician and surgeon licensed under the provisions of the Medicine Practice Act and to consent to an x-ray examination, anesthetic, dental or surgical diagnosis or treatment, and hospital care to be rendered to aid minor by a dentist licensed under the provisions of the Dental Practice Act.

It is understood that this authorization is given in advance of any specific diagnosis, treatment, or hospital care being required.

The above authorization is given pursuant to the provisions of the Civil Code of this state, section _____.

Photographic Release

We also give _____ /do not give _____ (initial one) our consent to _____ Church to photograph the above named person and, without limitation, to use such pictures and/or stories in connection with any work of said church and do _____ /do not _____ (initial one) hereby release said church from any claims whatsoever which may arise with regard thereto.

Signature of Parents or Legal Guardians:

Date _____ Signature _____

I have read, understand, and agree with the above statement as it applies to me.

Signature of Participant (18 years or older):

Date _____ Signature _____

Personal Physician _____

Accident/Health Insurance Co. _____
Policy No. _____

EVALUATION

To determine the effectiveness of any endeavor, we must set objectives. Engstrom and Dayton state in their book *Strategy for Living:*

> We need to start with purposes in our lives. We need great visions, grand dreams, great faith. But God expects us to take our faith a step further and set goals—statements that are measurable and accomplishable.
>
> A purpose, then, is an aim or direction, something which we want to achieve, but something which is not necessarily measurable.
>
> A goal, on the other hand, is a future event which we believe is both accomplishable and measurable. Measurable in terms of what is to be done, and how long it takes to do it.[4]

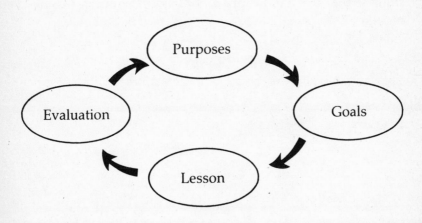

Purposes should be developed for Special Ministry programs. Specific goals can then be written to assist the teachers in accomplishing the purposes.

Two important cautions are in order:

- It takes an experienced teacher to set realistic goals with mentally retarded and deaf students. If goals are not realized initially, perhaps they were unrealistic. Teachers must continually evaluate their goals and lessons in light of new knowledge and insights.

- On the other hand, do not become a slave to goals. Goals are merely tools for directing our teaching toward the attainment of a purpose. The goal may change altogether or be modified by future circumstances.

TOTAL MINISTRY

Ministries to the disabled community should not be compartmentalized. Disabled persons should have the same opportunities as their nondisabled colleagues.

The chart on the next page suggests needs of persons with various disabilities. A dot is placed in categories where a special program is recommended. When a category is not marked, we suggest that the handicapped population be mainstreamed into regular classrooms.

Program	Behavior Disorders	Learning Disabilities	Physically Handicapped	Deaf	Blind	Mentally Handicapped	Category
Bible Study	•			•			Worship/Edification
Sunday School Class	•			•		•	Worship/Edification
Materials Center		•		•	•		Worship/Edification
Special Ministries Assistants	•	•	•	•	•	•	Worship/Edification
Discipleship	•	•	•	•	•		Worship/Edification
Special Friend Program	•		•	•	•	•	Recreation
Camping	•			•		•	Recreation
Special Events				•	•	•	Recreation
Individual and Team Sports			•			•	Recreation
Respite Care	•		•	•		•	Family
Family Counseling	•	•	•	•	•	•	Family
Family Day Outings	•		•	•		•	Family
Parent Classes	•	•	•	•	•	•	Family
Institutional Evangelism			•			•	Outreach
Vacation Bible School	•		•	•		•	Outreach
Workshops			•	•	•	•	Special Education
Learning Center	•	•	•	•	•	•	Special Education
Therapy Center			•				Special Education
School						•	Special Education
Transportation			•		•	•	Trans.
Residence			•		•	•	Res.

Notes

Introduction

1. Robert Lovering, *Out of the Ordinary* (Phoenix: ARCS, 1985).

Chapter 1

1. J.I. Packer, *Knowing God* (Hodder, 1975), 92.
2. Gloria Hawley, "Gifts of Joy," in *Decision* (April 1978).

Chapter 2

1. Charles Swindoll, *Three Steps Forward, Two Steps Back* (Marshall Pickering, 1983).

Chapter 3

1. John MacArthur, Jr. *The Church: The Body of Christ* (Grand Rapids: Zondervan, 1973), 121.
2. Ibid., 121–22.

Chapter 6

1. Adapted from S.R. Silverman, "Hard of Hearing Children," in Davis, Hallowell, and S.R. Silverman, eds., *Hearing and Deafness* (New York: Holt, Rinehart, and Winston, 1960). Distributors: WB Saunders, Eastbourne, U.K.

Chapter 8

1. Roger Dyer, "Blindness – What Is It?" Available through Christian Fellowship for the Blind International, Pasadena, California.

Chapter 9

1. R.D. Carpenter, *Why Can't I Learn?* (Glendale, Calif.: Regal, 1974), 1.

Chapter 10

1. Edward R. Dayton and Ted W. Engstrom, *Strategy for Living* (Glendale, Calif.: Regal, 1976), 94.
2. J. Oswald Sanders, *Spiritual Leadership* (Marshall Pickering 1986), 82.
3. Howard Hendricks, *Heaven Help the Home* (Wheaton, Ill.: Victor, 1973), 21–22.
4. Dayton and Engstrom, *Strategy for Living*, 49.

Photo used by permission of Joni and Friends, Inc.

In preparation for the publication of *All God's Children* in the United Kingdom, several agencies assisted in the compilation of the resources presented herein. The authors, while grateful for the many hours spent in preparing these references, have little knowledge about any of the agencies, organizations, or denominations listed.

The reader should be advised, therefore, that <u>all resources are listed for information purposes only</u> and do not imply <u>endorsement</u>.

Before spiritual counsel is sought from Christian organizations, their Statement of Faith should be requested. The Statement of Faith for Joni and Friends is printed here as a reference:

We believe in . . .

1. The verbally inspired and inerrantly written revelation of God as originally given; and its reliable preservation by God as the sixty-six books of the Bible, the only infallible and authoritative rule of faith and conduct.

2. The infinite, personal God, one in essence, yet eternally existing in three persons – Father, Son, and Holy Spirit – each the same in power and glory; and His sovereign rule in creation, providence, redemption and judgment.

3. The direct and perfect creation of man in God's image, but also the universal subjection of all people to pain, sorrow, sin, guilt and death, due to Adam's sin of disobedience and their inability to overcome the sinful nature by good works.

4. The atonement of the Lord Jesus Christ, the Son of God, who became man by the virgin birth, and by His sinless life, substitutionary death, bodily resurrection, ascension into heaven, and unique intercession, has redeemed all who believe in Him alone for salvation.

5. The regeneration of the Holy Spirit, by whose indwelling justification is completed as the sinner is enabled to believe and repent, and by whom sanctification is being accomplished as the believer is enabled more and more to live a holy life for the glory and enjoyment of God.

6. The spiritual unity of believers, which is the Church, the Body of Christ; and which is particularly manifested in local congregations where, through preaching and sacraments and discipline, God ministers through believers to the lost, the saved, the sick, the suffering, and the disabled, according to their need and His own perfect will.

7. The visible and bodily return of the Lord Jesus Christ in power and glory; and the bodily resurrection of both the lost and the saved; the lost unto judgment and everlasting punishment, the saved unto the perfection of life and the full enjoyment of God forever.